Celtic
PIECED ILLUSIONS

KAREN COMBS

QUILTERS PLUS

American Quilter's Society

Located in Paducah, Kentucky, the American Quilter's Society (AQS) is dedicated to promoting the accomplishments of today's quilters. Through its publications and events, AQS strives to honor today's quiltmakers and their work and to inspire future creativity and innovation in quiltmaking.

Editor: Barbara Smith
Graphic Design: Lynda Smith
Cover Design: Michael Buckingham
Photography: Charles Lynch

Published by American Quilter's Society

Library of Congress Cataloging-in-Publication Data
Combs, Karen.
    Celtic pieced illusions / by Karen Combs.
        p. cm.
    Summary: "Create Celtic quilt designs from pieced patterns with two simple blocks. Learn more about use of color and color illusion, texture, and value. Piecing tips, pressing options and quilting ideas along with teaching tips and lesson plans for teachers and quilt show owners."--Provided by publisher.
    ISBN 1-57432-916-2
    1. Patchwork--Patterns. 2. Quilting--Patterns.
    3. Decoration and ornament, Celtic.
    I. American Quilter's Society. II. Title.
TT835.C6483 2006
746.46'041--dc22
                    2006029674

An Irish Blessing

May there always be work for your hands to do;

May your purse always hold a coin or two;

May the sun always shine on your windowpane;

May a rainbow be certain to follow each rain;

May the hand of a friend always be near you;

May God fill your heart with gladness to cheer you.

Additional copies of this book may be ordered from the American Quilter's Society, PO Box 3290, Paducah, KY 42002-3290; 800-626-5420 (orders only please); or online at www.AmericanQuilter.com. For all other inquiries, please call 270-898-7903.

Dedication

This book is dedicated to the many friendships I have made as I traveled the quilt world. To the students, teachers, and advisors who have changed my life forever, I thank you and wish you peace.

Acknowledgments

There are many people who supported and gave me encouragement while I wrote this book. I'd like to thank, in a special way ...

• my husband, Rick. Without your support and encouragement, I would not be living my dream.

• my children, Angela and Josh, for enriching my life.

• Terry Dramstad, whose machine quilting made my quilts shine. Thank you so much!

• Marjie Rhine, Lisa Newcomer, Claudia Sauer, Ellen White, Rachel Eby, Lyn Anderson, Teddy Wenner, Sally Catlin, Debi Tallerico, and Mary Phillips. Thank you for allowing me to use your creative adaptations. Your quilts and drawings add a sparkle to this book.

• all the students in my online Pieced Celtic Magic class at QuiltUniversity.com. For your excitement and encouragement about this technique, I thank you!

• the special people at the American Quilter's Society: Barbara Smith, whose editing skills and guidance make this project easier; Helen Squire and Jay Staten, for your dedicated efforts on my behalf; Bill and Meredith Schroeder and many others at the American Quilter's Society, for helping me make this project a reality.

• American & Efird, Inc., and Marci Brier for Mettler® and Signature® threads.

• Blank Quilting, in New York, for the fabric.

• Diana Mancini, Renee Burdette, and Billy Alper for their help, friendship, and going the extra mile. Creating fabric with you is a pleasure!

• Prym-Dritz/Omnigrid® for notions, rotary cutters, rulers, and mats.

• Superior Thread and Heather Purcell for thread.

Contents

Page 52

Page 88

Page 68

Page 80

Page 92

Page 96

Introduction

Celtic art involves the use of distinctive spirals, key patterns, stylized figures, and knot work. Celtic knot work consists of designs in which cords interlace to form decorative knots.

Traditional Corded Knots

Celtic knot work has ...*no loose ends.* At its purest, a cord is formed into loops that are interlaced into pleasing designs to fill a space. Historical examples often consist of a single endless loop. Many people suppose that this loop is symbolic of eternity, and it is certainly useful for contemplation as you follow the line around and around the pattern.

Symmetry. If the overall symmetry is ignored, knot work will resemble a plate of spaghetti. The symmetry comes from the pattern of overlapping loops made in the braided cord, making the cord appear to twist and turn like a roller coaster. The symmetry can take several forms (see figures below):

Rotation – The pattern rotates around a point.
Reflection – The pattern contains one or more lines of symmetry in the pattern of overlaps.
Translation – The pattern is offset and repeated.

Consistent interlacing. The cords should always interlace consistently. That is, when you follow a line, if it goes over one cord, then it will go under the next cord it intersects, and then over, and so on. The cord of a loop isn't split, and no more than two cords ever meet at any intersection. If you ignore these restrictions, lacing consistency is difficult to achieve.

Rotation

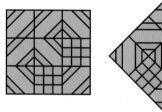 

The pattern rotates around a point.

Reflection (mirror image)

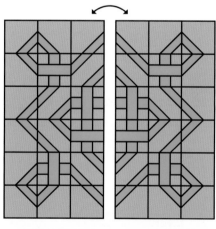

The pattern is the mirror images of the opposite side.

Consistent cord width. For nearly all knot-work panels, the cord width is kept consistent. Some may argue that the width of the cords should be equal to the gap between the cords, but this rule is not always used in historical examples.

Pieced Knots

Celtic Patchwork Illusions was born from my love of geometric designs, such as knot gardens and Celtic art. Several years ago, when I traveled to Scotland and England, I was intrigued by the beautiful Celtic knot work I saw on buildings, crosses, and stonework.

I wanted to use these designs as inspiration for Celtic designs of my own creation but was not sure how to do it. Quilters traditionally use appliqué to create Celtic designs, and while I love the look of appliquéd Celtic work, I prefer making pieced quilts. I decided to play with these designs and try to work out a piecing method. After considerable time, I came up with a fantastic method. By using only two simple blocks, I found that I could create Celtic designs and that unlimited designs were possible.

I am honored to share these exciting aspects of Celtic design with you. If you enjoy designing your own quilt, I will show you how to do just that in chapter one. I'll also show you how to use color, texture, and value to add exciting illusions to your Celtic quilts. I will walk you through a number of different exercises so you can fully explore the design options before you ever cut a piece of fabric. When your quilt is finished, it will truly be your own design.

If you enjoy making quilts from patterns, I've included several patterns for beautiful quilts that you can make. No matter what you prefer, there is something for you in Celtic Patchwork Illusions.

Translation

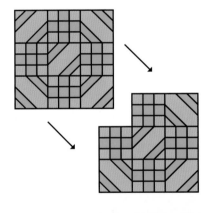

The pattern is moved sideways and repeated.

Chapter 1

Let's Play

Building Blocks

All the quilts are made from two basic blocks: the Nine-Patch and the Connector block. It may be hard to believe, but it is true! All the designs you will see in this chapter and in following chapters can be made with these two blocks. With a twist and a turn, a new design is created. It's magic!

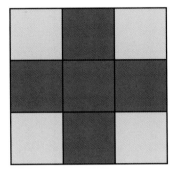 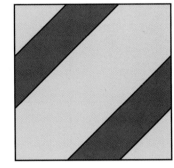

Fig. 1. Nine-Patch block   *Connector block*

Simple Grid

We are going to start by working with a simple grid, six blocks by six blocks, and the two basic blocks. Print out several copies of the grid on page 10. You will need Nine-Patch and Connector blocks to fill in the grid, so also print out several copies of the blocks on page 11.

Yes, I know the blocks are in black and white and may seem boring. Don't worry; we will be working with color later. However, at first, I want you to work in black and white only. Okay, I know it's really light gray and white, not black and white. There is a reason for the light gray rather than black. Later, we will be adding color in our designs, and it's easier to color over light gray than black.

Why are we using black and white rather than color? I'm glad you asked! When designing a quilt, I have found that color can be distracting. I often work on my initial design in black and white. By doing this, I can see the "bones" of the design; that is, I can see the design in its purest form without color getting in the way. Once I have worked out a pleasing design in black and white, I can add color. Color will enhance a good design, but it will never save a poor one.

All right, grab your glue stick and your paper scissors. I like using a removable glue stick so the blocks can be repositioned. I found my glue stick at a chain office-supply store. If you can't find this type of glue stick, you can select another brand. However, use very little glue and press the blocks down lightly. You will need to be able to move them around.

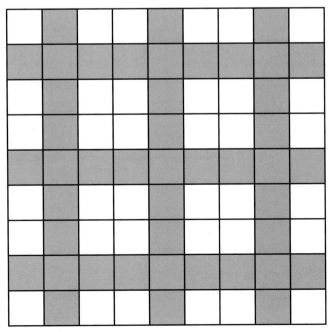

Nine-Patch blocks

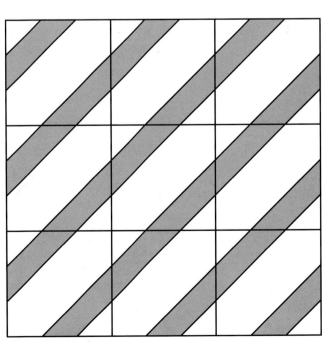

Connector blocks

Let's Play

Block Grid
Copy this grid as needed to play with your blocks.

Blocks to Play With
Make copies of the blocks and cut them out.

Nine-Patch Blocks **Connector Blocks** **Modified Connector Blocks**

Let's Play

Playing with Blocks

Place 16 Nine-Patch blocks on the grid as shown in figure 2. Don't skip ahead and put the Connector blocks in, just place the Nine-Patch blocks into the grid.

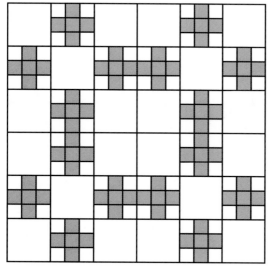

Fig. 2. Place Nine-Patch blocks first.

At this point, it doesn't look like much, but just wait. The Connector blocks will make the magic happen. Now, place 20 Connector blocks on the grid (fig. 3). Wow! Isn't it amazing! I love seeing the change between the first illustration and this one.

Fig. 3. Add Connector blocks.

You have just created one version of a Celtic pieced illusion quilt. It looks similar to an ancient Celtic knot design, but it is much easier to create.

Variation

The design we have just created is wonderful, but it's just the start. Let me show you how easy it is to create many different designs.

Look at figure 4. The only block rotated is one middle block. Look at the change! This is the magic at work. By rotating the Connector blocks, you can create numerous designs.

Fig. 4. Rotating one block changes the design.

Let's create a new design in the center by rotating all four center blocks as shown in figure 5. The interlocked braid has been changed into an octagon shape. Now, the center design no longer echoes the corners. This is an easy way to change a design.

Fig. 5. Rotated center blocks

Let's go one step further. Rotate the corner blocks as shown in figure 6. Instead of closing the corner with a strip that crosses the corner, we are opening a path.

Fig. 6. Rotated corner blocks

I find this absolutely fascinating. We have only rotated the inner four blocks and the four corners, but the design is totally different.

More Variations

Notice that, in the following variations, the designs are created by rotating only the Connector blocks. In figure 7, the design has many woven and overlapping sections. The corners are turned on the diagonal, and this helps lead your eye around the edges of the quilt.

Fig. 7. Variation

The first design in figure 8 is good, but the top-left corner and bottom-right corner lead the eye out of the design. I like the second design much better. The top-left corner and the bottom-right corner have been turned, which creates interlocking circles.

Fig. 8. Good

Better

The design in figure 9 is similar to the previous one; however, the center four blocks have been turned to create an on-point square, which feels more open.

Fig. 9. Even better

Exercise 1

Now it's your turn to play. Take the six-by-six grid (page 10) and the Nine-Patch and Connector blocks you have cut out and create different designs. Work with only this grid and these blocks. We will be looking at other options in the following exercises.

Exercise 2

For this exercise, we will also start with a six-by-six grid. You may also need to print out more blocks. Place the Nine-Patch blocks as shown in figure 10.

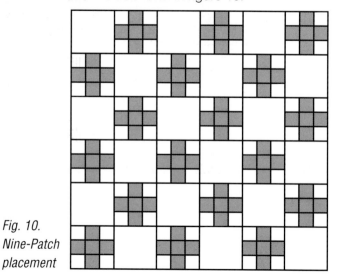

Fig. 10. Nine-Patch placement

Let's add the Connector blocks and make some magic happen. Place all the Connector blocks going in the same direction, which creates a beautiful chain or braid (fig. 11).

Fig. 11. Add Connector blocks.

In one of my online classes, student Claudia Sauer created two appealing braid designs with this exercise (fig. 12). In the first variation, she finished off the braid by adding more pieces around the outside edge. In her second variation, she rotated the center Connector blocks to create in interesting open area in the braid.

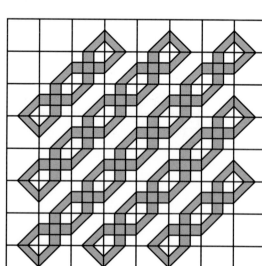

Fig. 12. Variation 1

Variation 2

For the next example, rotate the Connector blocks to create an interlocking chain (fig. 13). I'm always amazed how this simple change can create a totally different design.

*Fig. 13.
Interlocking
chain*

Now it's your turn. For this exercise, play with the blocks and create different designs. Take your time and you will be surprised at the designs you can make. Stay with the black-and-white blocks ... no color yet.

Exercise 3

In this exercise, we are going add more Connector blocks to the designs. Start by printing out a blank six-by-six grid (page 10). Place Nine-Patch blocks into the grid as shown in figure 14.

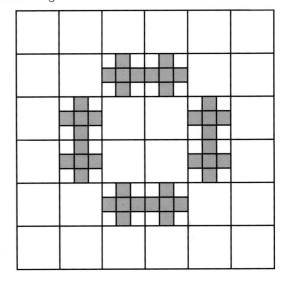

*Fig. 14.
Nine-Patch
placement*

Looks empty, doesn't it? Well, let's fix that. Place Connector blocks into the grid as shown in figure 15. Isn't it fantastic? This design reminds me of an English knot garden.

*Fig. 15.
English
knot garden*

Chapter 4

Let's Play

Let's create new designs by rotating the Connector blocks (fig. 16). In class, Claudia created a beautiful interlocking design by rotating the outer Connector blocks. Lisa Newcomer then rotated the center Connector blocks to create a totally different design.

If the inner and outer Connector blocks are turned, paths can be created that lead the eye out of the design. If the inner blocks are turned in this design, the beautiful ring in the center becomes the focus (fig. 17).

Fig. 16. Claudia's version

Fig. 17. Version with paths

Lisa's version

Version with center ring

Let's do a few more and see that happens. Four repeating motifs are created in this option (fig. 18). Although the edges are unfinished, your eye is still led around the design. If you like this version, see what happens when four of these designs are put together. A complex, yet beautiful, pattern is created.

I love the interwoven lines in the center of this design, which reminds me of a Log Cabin setting (fig. 19).

Fig 19. Woven center motif with open edges

Fig. 18. Four motifs

Sixteen motifs

Log Cabin setting

Here are some more fun variations. Rachel Eby created a design with a lovely woven braid in the center, and Mary Phillips created a diagonal braid. I've removed the Connector blocks to make it easier to see the designs (fig. 20).

Fig. 20. Rachel's design

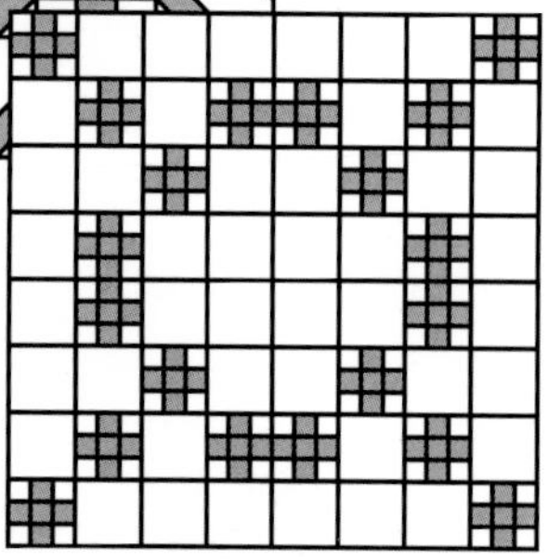

Rachel's design minus Connector blocks

Mary's design

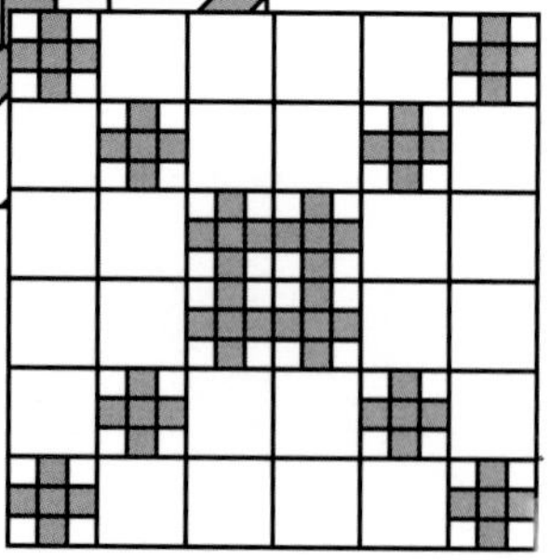

Mary's design minus Connector blocks

Your turn! In this exercise, play with different designs that contain more Connector than Nine-Patch blocks.

Exercise 4

For this exercise, we are going to continue working with the six-by-six grid and the Nine-Patch block. However, we are going to modify the Connector block by removing one corner (fig. 21). This will give us even more design options.

Fig. 21.   Connector block   Modified Connector block

Print a blank six-by-six grid, (page 10) and a page of modified Connector blocks (page 11). Also print more Nine-Patch blocks if needed.

Okay, let's play! Start with the same Log-Cabin-like design (fig 22), then insert modified Connector blocks in the corners (fig. 23). Look at the difference! You can use this block to create new open spaces in your designs.

Fig. 22. Log-Cabin-like design

Fig. 23. Modified Connector blocks added to corners

Now, move the modified Connector blocks to the center of each side of the quilt and rotate three Connector blocks in each corner to form circles. This makes a totally different design (fig. 24).

Fig. 24. More open design

You can create woven braids by using even more Nine-Patch blocks. It is easy to do. Start with a six-by-six grid and add Nine-Patch blocks as shown in figure 25. Add Modified Connector blocks to two corners and Connector blocks to the other spaces to make woven braids.

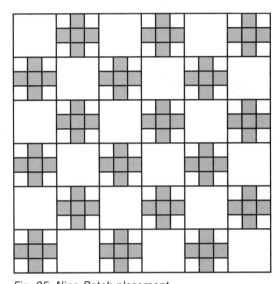

Fig. 25. Nine-Patch placement

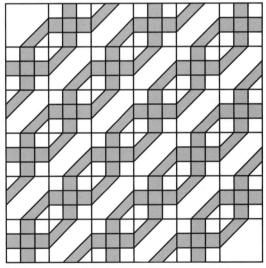

Add connector blocks to make woven braids.

As we have worked with the different exercises, you may have noticed that some of the designs were cut off around the edges. You may like that effect, as we saw in the Log Cabin design in figure 19. However, you may want to finish off the design. This is a great option you can explore. I like to start by adding a row of empty squares around the entire design (fig. 26).

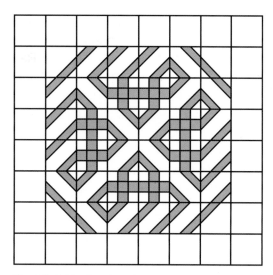

Fig. 26. Add a border of empty squares.

Now I can add blocks around the edge and finish off the design. Most of the time, I use Modified Connector blocks. If I used the Nine-Patch block or the Connector block, it would extend the design rather than finish it (fig. 27).

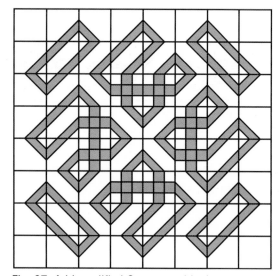

Fig. 27. Add modified Connector blocks.

I like this version, but I think it can be better. By turning a few blocks in the center, I can create another look. I like this option much better, with its open areas and the twisted designs in the center (fig. 28). As you work with your designs, do not be afraid to finish them off with another round of blocks.

Fig. 28. A more interesting design

For exercise four, play with the Modified Connector blocks as well as the Connector blocks and Nine-Patches. Try many different combinations and see what you come up with.

Grid Options

There is one more idea I want to give you. To make designing easy to understand, I have given you a six-by-six grid. I have found this grid gives us many options, yet it is easy to play with as you rotate your blocks.

However, you can use many different grids. Some of my favorites are six by six, eight by eight, and ten by ten. I've even played with a fourteen-by-fourteen grid with fantastic results. As you increase the grid size, you increase the complexity of the designs. Notice that the last design in figure 29 has empty squares. This gives you one more design option.

Fig. 29. Eight-by-eight grid

To make grids in any size you want, just print several copies of the six-by-six grid and tape together however many you need. This will keep the squares the same size as your little blocks. If you make a design that is symmetrical in fourths, like the last design in figure 1–28, you can create one fourth of the design and just copy and rotate it to complete the design.

If you are interested in creating your own Celtic patchwork illusions quilts, set aside designs that you love. You can choose from these designs to make a quilt. Remember, the more complex the design, the longer it will take to make. That may be a consideration as you work. If you want to start with an easier design, stay with a six-by-six grid. Your design will be beautiful and won't take long to create. If you want to create an incredible, complex design, work with a twelve-by-twelve or a fourteen-by-fourteen grid (fig. 30). It will take longer, but it will be fantastic!

Ten-by-ten grid

Fig. 30. Fourteen-by-fourteen grid

Fourteen-by-fourteen grid

Chapter 2

Color & Value

Color & Value

Did you take some time to play with the basic blocks? Did you start to see them in your sleep? Sometimes this happens to me, when I am designing quilts. It's fun to dream up some interesting combinations.

After working with only black-and-white blocks, I know you are ready to add some color to your designs. In this chapter, we will add colors to the quilts and use color to create illusions. We have a lot to cover, so let's get started.

There are many options when selecting fabrics for these quilts. Before we look at color combinations, I want to share some basic color information with you. It will help as you start playing with colors and deciding what to use in your quilt.

Color Temperature

Colors have temperature. While it is not a temperature you can feel, it is something you can view and sense. It is a visual illusion, but it is something we need to consider before selecting fabrics. Colors are either warm or cool in temperature—visual temperature that is (fig. 1).

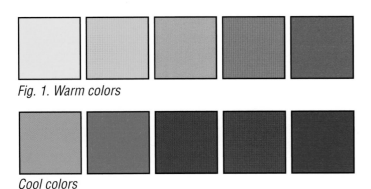

Fig. 1. Warm colors

Cool colors

Warm colors are the ones you see in fire: yellow, yellow-orange, orange, red-orange, and red. These colors are exciting to use. They have energy. They can stimulate the senses, and they visually advance. Cool colors are the ones you see in water: blue, blue-green, violet, and blue-violet. These colors are calming and restful. They can be pleasing to use, and they visually recede.

Warm Colors

If you want to make a stimulating quilt, use warm colors or very bright colors. The quilt in figure 2 is a good example. It combines the warm, bright colors of deep red and bright orange. This combination is lively and filled with energy.

Fig. 2. Quilt design with all warm colors

Exercise 1

Play with this concept. Select one of your designs and color it in with warm, stimulating colors. Or, you can use the line drawing below for this exercise. Make several copies of the drawing, because we will use it for several exercises.

Fig. 3. Copy and color line drawing

Color & Value

Cool Colors

If you want a quilt that is calmer, use cool or dull colors. The quilt in figure 4 is a good example of cool, soft colors. A medium-value purple and a grayed blue create a calming look that resembles the colors of a cool spring morning. The blue background is slightly lighter than the purple, which helps define the Celtic knot work. Consider how light or dark the colors are as you fill in your designs.

Fig. 4. Quilt design with all cool colors.

Exercise 2

Play with this concept—select one of your designs or use the line drawing and color it in with cool, calming colors. Create several variations. I'm sure you will be surprised at the difference in the quilts from the first two exercises.

Combined Temperatures

Many quilts have a combination of warm and cool colors (fig. 5). I love this option because it creates the best of both color worlds. There's the energy of a warm color with the calming effect of a cool color. Using warm and cool colors can also help define a background or the knot work in a quilt.

Fig. 5. Quilt design with warm and cool colors

Exercise 3

Play with this idea—select one of your designs or use the line drawing from figure 3 and color it in with warm and cool colors. Experiment. You will love the quilts you can create!

As you select colors for your quilts, think about the mood that warm and cool colors can suggest. In selecting fabrics for a quilt, I often ask myself what type of quilt I want to make. A calm, peaceful quilt? If so, I use cool colors. An energetic quilt? If so, I use warm colors. A combination of both color temperatures? These questions will help you as you select the colors for your quilt.

Color Value

Color is the first thing you may think about when selecting fabric for a quilt. You may find yourself agonizing over colors and asking yourself, "Does this blue go with that red? Can yellow be added to this quilt?" You may be amazed to learn that value and texture are often more important than color. Surprising, isn't it! In most quilts, color gets all the credit, while value and texture do all the work.

What Is Value?

You may be asking, "What exactly is value?" It is the lightness and darkness of a fabric. Quilts often need light, medium, and dark values to create an exciting design. If a quilt does not have different values, the design can be boring. Quilts will vary in their value needs. Some need medium and light values, some need light and dark values, while others need a variety.

For example, the design in figure 6 has cool colors in light teal, medium blue, and dark purple. I've added a twist. Notice the light teal background. This is a batik that combines smudges of yellow along with the teal. I love to use batiks that have a touch of another color in them. Because teal is a cool color, the touch of yellow, a warm color, creates interest in the design.

Fig. 7. The yellow center echoes the yellow frame.

Fig. 6. Cool colors with a bit of lemon.

The lovely example in figure 7 has warm and cool colors in a variety of values. The warm color is a light yellow. The cool colors are light teal, medium teal, light blue, and medium-dark blue. Let's look at how these colors are placed in the design. I wanted to emphasize the background. Because warm colors draw your eyes, I placed yellow in the background in the center of the quilt. Do you see the on-point square that is created? This is exactly what I intended, and yellow helps this happen.

I have used my batik trick in other parts of the background as well. The same light teal and yellow batik was used in the corners, along with a darker piece that has teal and blue. Fabrics that incorporate two colors help tie the parts of the quilt together.

Notice also the Celtic cross (fig. 8). I wanted to emphasize this part of the center design, and using a darker blue fabric provides the needed contrast.

Fig. 8. The medium blue brings out the Celtic cross.

Color & Value

Determining Value

Many quilters are unsure about value and therefore stick with medium values. While this may feel safe, it does not make for an exciting design. Some quilters may be afraid of value because they are unsure whether a fabric is light, medium, or dark. Here are a few tricks to help you determine the value of a fabric.

Value is relative to its neighboring fabrics. The following demonstration will help you understand how value is determined:

When this fabric is by itself, it appears light.

However, when a lighter fabric is placed next to it, the first fabric appears darker.

When a very dark fabric is laid next to the first fabric, it appears light again.

 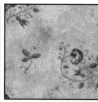 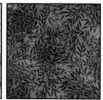

When placed between a lighter and a darker fabric, the first fabric reads as medium in value.

A value finder can help you determine the value of a fabric. There are several on the market. This tool takes away color and turns it into a grayscale, which shows the relative lightness or darkness of the fabric.

The red value tool will work on all colors except red. When you are determining the value of red fabrics, use the green value tool. The green value tool will work on all colors except green. To determine the value of green fabrics, use the red value tool. Consequently, you will need both the red and the green value finders as you work with different fabrics.

If you have a multicolored fabric, overlap the tools and use them together. When placed together, they create a brownish color, and this will work on almost every fabric color. You may find using both tools together makes everything look a bit dark, but you will still be able to see through them.

To use the value tools, select several fabrics whose values puzzle you. Place them next to each other or slightly overlap them. Put the tool up to your eyes and look through the tool. The fabric should appear light or dark, almost black or white. You can now tell which fabric is lighter (fig. 9).

Fig. 9. Fabrics viewed without a value tool

Viewed through the red tool

Viewed through the green tool

Viewed through both green and red tools

Some quilters have trouble using a value tool. Usually, it's because they are laying the value finder on the fabric instead of putting it up to their eyes. If, in the past, you have had trouble with value finders, give this a try.

Exercise 4
Now you can play with values. Use the line drawing on page 23 or one of your own drawings. Be sure to try light, medium, and dark values as well as warm and cool colors in the drawing.

Transparency

Value can be used to create exciting illusions, such as the appearance of overlapping cords. It is easy to do, yet it produces the optical illusion of dimension. Transparency is the illusion of layers that you can see through. It appears that you have taken one piece of fabric and laid it on top of another, but you can still see through to the bottom fabric (fig. 10).

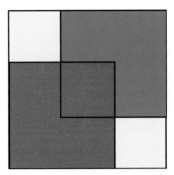

Fig. 10. Overlapping, with no transparency

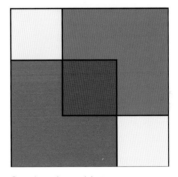

Overlapping with transparency

A cable design is a perfect place to add the illusion of transparency. Let me show you an example. Figure 11 shows a cable design without transparency. Notice that each cord is a different color, teal and purple. However, they are similar in value. This is important: for the illusion to happen, use a different color for each cord but keep them similar in value.

Fig. 11. Without transparency

Now for the magic! I can add transparency into the square patch where the cords overlap. By using a darker value of each color, I can make the cords appear woven and transparent (fig. 12).

Fig. 12. With transparency

Notice the placement of the darker values and see how it creates the illusion of transparency. I have used a darker purple and a darker teal. By alternating the darker squares, the cords appear interwoven and transparent.

If you want transparency in your quilt, use the following guidelines:

• Use different colors for the cords. Make sure the colors coordinate well with each other, such as blue and green.

• Keep the cords similar in value. Select light to medium values for the braids, not dark ones.

• Use a darker value of each color to create the transparency.

• Alternating the dark values will create a woven effect.

• Use non-busy prints.

Exercise 5

The best way to understand transparency is to play with it. Experiment and create several different designs with transparency.

Now you can put everything in this lesson to use. Try using warm and cool colors. Select different values for your designs. Try out ideas you think will work and try out some combinations that may appear odd. You will be amazed by your designs.

Texture

Before you start selecting fabrics for your quilt, we need to look at fabric texture. Texture refers to a visual texture, or the pattern in a fabric. It does not refer to a texture you can feel. I have found that Celtic illusions work best with non-busy prints.

Busy prints have many colors or strong contrast within the print. The pattern may be large or small in scale (fig. 13).

Fig.13. Busy prints

Non-busy prints generally have low contrast, fewer colors, and more subtle patterns (fig. 14). From a distance, these prints often appear as solid colors. However, they can add more depth and richness to a quilt than a flat, solid-colored fabric.

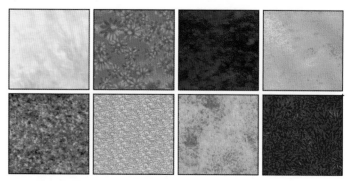

Fig. 14. Non-busy prints

Let me show you some examples of busy and non-busy prints in quilts. The quilt in figure 15 contains two busy fabrics. Each fabric has a lot of visual texture, and the two textures are fighting each other. While the overall design is visible, it is not easy to see, so these fabrics are not the best choice.

Fig. 15. Busy fabrics fight each other and blur the design.

In the quilt in figure 16, I changed the lighter busy fabric to a non-busy dark blue and changed the darker busy print to a non-busy green. This combination is more pleasing. The design is clear, and the fabrics are not fighting each other.

Fig. 16. Busy prints combined with non-busy fabrics create a pleasing design.

In figure 17, I switched the position of the fabrics. The non-busy fabric is now in the background, and the busy fabric is in the woven cords. Exchanging the fabrics creates a different look. I love both of them and am always fascinated by this option.

Fig. 17. Fabrics switched

As you select fabrics for your quilt, remember to consider their visual texture. If the fabrics are too busy, your design will not be apparent and the fabrics will "mush" together. I prefer using non-busy fabrics for Celtic quilts, because I enjoy seeing the design clearly displayed.

Inspiration

As you design your own quilts, you can use some of the
following student designs as inspiration:

*Debi Tallerico's design combines warm and cool colors in
charming interlocking hearts.*

This intricate design by Sally Catlin has a unique woven effect.

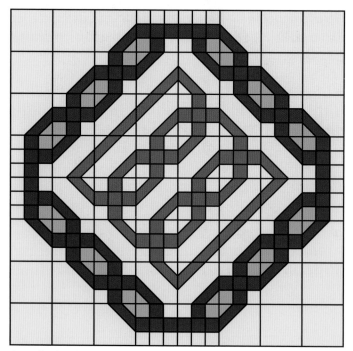

*Lyn Anderson's design combines warm and cool colors to
create a Celtic design with the look of stained glass.*

*Mary Phillips used cool colors to create a beautiful transparent
design.*

Teddy Wenner has used warm colors outlined in black for her striking design.

CHAPTER 3

From Design to Fabric

Determining Quilt Size

First things first—you need to decide on a size for your quilt. Whenever I am trying to decide on a size, I ask myself the following questions:

What is the function of the quilt? Will it be a wallhanging, table runner, throw, baby quilt, or bed quilt? Once I have decided on the function, I can decide on the size. The most common size I use for a wallhanging is between 36" and 45" square. The size of your wallhanging will, of course, be determined by your wall space. A throw is also a popular quilt to make. A common throw size is approximately 45" x 63".

If you have chosen to make a bed quilt, the following chart lists common mattress sizes. It shows the measurements for the mattress tops only, not down the sides. To make a quilt that covers the sides, keep in mind that new mattresses are much thicker than old ones. So are the box springs.

Common Matress Sizes

Crib	27" x 52"	Queen	60" x 80"
Twin	39" x 75"	King	72" x 84"
Full	54" x 75"		

Bed Quilt Size Chart

I use the following form to help me determine the size of a bed quilt. You may want to use it, too. Just fill in the blanks with your measurements.

Bed Quilt Size	Width	Length
Mattress dimensions	_____"	_____"
Add drop		
right side	_____"	
left side	_____"	
bottom		_____"
Add to cover pillows		_____"
Add for shrinkage*	_____"	_____"
*See Causes of Shrinkage in the next column		
Total (ideal quilt size)	_____"	_____"

Causes of Shrinkage

There are three things that can cause shrinkage in your quilt:

- If you did not prewash, you can lose two to four percent in overall size when you wash your quilt. This amount needs to be added to both quilt dimensions.

- Quilting by hand or machine will also cause your quilt to shrink. Experience is your best guide as to how much your quilting style causes this to happen. This amount needs to be added to both dimensions.

- You need to consider that, when you sleep on your side, the quilt lifts up an amount equal to double the width of your body. If you have a partner, that amount should be figured in as well. The object is for the quilt to adequately cover anyone who normally sleeps in the bed. This amount would affect only the width of your quilt.

How Many Blocks?

Once you know the size of your quilt, you need to decide what block size to use. Your first consideration is scale. If you are making a wall quilt, you will want to use small blocks, which will look appropriate in a small space. For a bed quilt, you will want to use large blocks because they will look more in scale with a large project.

Your second consideration is the design you have chosen. You need to be sure that all the elements of your design can be completed in the space available.

As a third consideration, some quilt designs work better if laid out in an odd number of rows with an odd number of blocks across the rows. This would be a compelling consideration in choosing both the number of blocks and their size.

Once you know your ideal quilt size and the block size you want to use, here's how to determine the number of blocks you will need: divide the block size into both the length and width of your ideal quilt size. This will give you the number of blocks across and down the quilt, as shown in the following examples.

From Design to Fabric

Example 1   Quilt size 72" x 90"
Finished block size 9"
$$72" \div 9" = 8$$
$$90" \div 9" = 10$$

This quilt is 8 blocks by 10 blocks, 80 blocks total, but what happens if your division produces an uneven number?

Example 2   Quilt size 72" x 90"
Finished block size 12"
$$72" \div 12" = 6$$
$$90" \div 12" = 7.5$$

This quilt is 6 blocks by 7½ blocks, so you can choose a different block size, or you can use 7 blocks and add additional borders to make up the difference.

Building Blocks

Before cutting fabric, figure out how many of each block you need and what colors they will be. Make a color chart for each block. Looking at the sample quilt design in figure 1, there are only three different blocks.

make 20   make 8   make 8

Fig. 1. Sample quilt 1 and block chart

Let's look at the more complex design in figure 2. This quilt is the same design as in figure 1, but it has more colors. Let's analyze this quilt to see what blocks are needed.

make 8   make 12   make 8   make 8

Fig. 2. Sample quilt 2 and block color chart

Sometimes, I become confused as to how many of each block there are. Here is a double check that is helpful. Look at the empty grid and count the total number of blocks. In the sample quilt, it's 36. Then add up the number of blocks of each type in the design. The total should also equal 36.

Look at your design and examine it to establish the number of blocks of each type. On page 35. you will find a Quilt Design Worksheet that will help you analyze your quilt and determine the number of blocks to make.

Quilt Design Worksheet

Copy this page as needed for your quilt designs.

Quilt size: Block size:

Paste finished quilt design here.

Block Color Chart

Color the blocks, as needed, to match your quilt design.

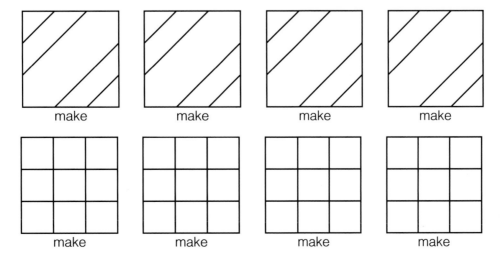

make   make   make   make

make   make   make   make

From Design to Fabric

What Do I Cut?

Once you have worked out the number of blocks you need and their colorations, you can use the following chart to determine the size to cut the patches in each block.

Cutting Patches

Nine-Patch

Block size	3"	6"	9"
Cut	1½"	2½"	3½"

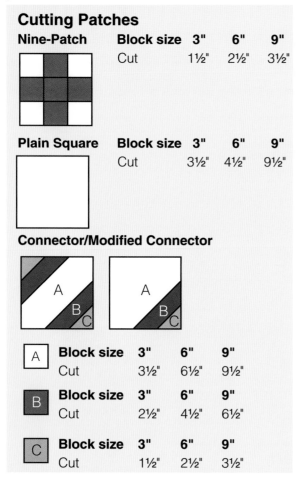

Plain Square

Block size	3"	6"	9"
Cut	3½"	4½"	9½"

Connector/Modified Connector

A	Block size	3"	6"	9"
	Cut	3½"	6½"	9½"

B	Block size	3"	6"	9"
	Cut	2½"	4½"	6½"

C	Block size	3"	6"	9"
	Cut	1½"	2½"	3½"

Sample Quilt

Let me show you the cutting needs for sample quilt 1. Refer to the Sample Cutting Chart for 6" Blocks to the right and follow along as I walk you through the steps.

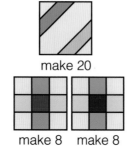

make 20

make 8   make 8

Sample Cutting Chart for 6" Blocks

Based on fabric at least 40" wide. Cut strips selvage to selvage.

Color/Block/Patch	First Cut	Second Cut
Tan Connector block, patch A	(4) strips 6½"	(20) squares 6½"
Tan Connector block patch C	(3) strips 2½"	(40) squares 2½"
Tan Nine-patch	(4) strips 2½"	(64) squares 2½"
Light blue Connector block, patch B	(3) strips 4½"	(20) squares 4½"
Light blue Nine-patch	(2) strips 2½"	(32) squares 2½"
Dark blue Nine-patch	(1) strip 2½"	(8) squares 2½"
Light green Connector block patch B	(3) strips 4½"	(20) squares 4½"
Light green Nine-patch	(2) strips 2½"	(32) squares 2½"
Dark green Nine-patch	(1) strip 2½"	(8) squares 2½"

Steps for filling in chart

1. In the table heading, fill in the block size on the line.

2. In column 1, fill in the colors, blocks, and patches.

3. For columns 2 and 3, refer to the Cutting Patches chart on this page to fill in the cut size for each patch on the line. Because the patches are square, the size will be the same for both columns.

4. For each entry in column 1, count the number of patches needed. Enter the numbers in the parentheses in column 3.

5. Determine how many strips need to be cut, which is a two-step process:

  a. Divide the fabric width (use 40") by the patch width. We will use the first row of the Sample Cutting Chart above as our example:

  40" fabric width ÷ 6½" (patch A) = 6.15 patches per strip. Therefore 6 whole patches can be cut from one strip.

b. Divide the number of patches needed by the number of patches that can be cut from one strip.

20 squares ÷ 6 patches per strip = 3.33 strips which is 4 whole strips. Enter these numbers in the parentheses in column 2.

Why 40" Fabric Width?

Good question! I find that many so-called 44"–45" fabrics are considerably narrower. Also, the selvages can be quite wide and need to be removed. In addition, if you prewash your fabrics, they can shrink as much as five percent. Therefore, it's safest to use 40" as your fabric width when calculating yardage.

Now it's time for you to fill out your Cutting Chart at right. Be sure to have your quilt drawing, quilt design chart, and cutting patches chart in front of you. You will need all this information to fill out your cutting chart. Follow the steps as I have described. If you try to skip around, you won't be able to work out your cutting needs.

*Copy this page as needed
for your quilt designs.*

Cutting Chart for _____" Blocks

Color/Block/Patch	First Cut	Second Cut
	( ) strips ____"	( ) squares ____"
	( ) strips ____"	( ) squares ____"
	( ) strips ____"	( ) squares ____"
	( ) strips ____"	( ) squares ____"
	( ) strips ____"	( ) squares ____"
	( ) strips ____"	( ) squares ____"
	( ) strips ____"	( ) squares ____"
	( ) strips ____"	( ) squares ____"
	( ) strips ____"	( ) squares ____"
	( ) strips ____"	( ) squares ____"
	( ) strips ____"	( ) squares ____"
	( ) strips ____"	( ) squares ____"
	( ) strips ____"	( ) squares ____"
	( ) strips ____"	( ) squares ____"
	( ) strips ____"	( ) squares ____"
	( ) strips ____"	( ) squares ____"
	( ) strips ____"	( ) squares ____"

Figuring Yardage

How did it go? Did you fill in your chart? Great! Do you realize how much you have learned so far? I'm so proud of you.

Now you can figure out your yardage needs. Again, we will look at the Cutting Chart for the sample quilt on page 36, and I'll walk you through the steps.

Steps for figuring yardage

1. Write down each color in your quilt design.
   Tan
   Light blue
   Dark blue
   Light green
   Dark green

2. Working with one color at a time, multiply the number of strips by the patch size to find the number of inches needed.
   Tan
   4 strips x 6½" patch size = 26"
   3 strips x 2½" patch size = 7.5"
   4 strips x 2½" patch size = 10"

3. Add the inches from each line together.
   26" + 7.5" + 10" = 43.5" of fabric

4. To find the yardage, divide 43.5" by 36", which is the number of inches in a yard.
   43.5" ÷ 36" = 1.2 yards

However, what if you make a cutting mistake? Also, there's the matter of shrinkage if you prewash. When figuring yardage, I like to round up. In this case, I would buy at least 1¼ yards or even 1⅓ yards.

5. Continue your calculations until the yardage for each color has been determined. Here are the yardages for the sample quilt.

Fabric	Yards
Tan	1⅓
Light blue	⅝
Dark blue	¼
Light green	⅝
Dark green	¼

Inches to Yards Conversion Chart

Inches		Yards
4½"	=	⅛
9"	=	¼
12"	=	⅓
13½"	=	⅜
18"	=	½
22½"	=	⅝
24"	=	⅔
27"	=	¾
31½"	=	⅞
36"	=	1

CHAPTER 4

Sewing Hints

Let's look at the sewing sequence for each block. I know you are interested in the Connector block—just how are we going to make it with only squares?

Connector Block

For each Connector block, you will have three different sizes of squares: A, B, and C (fig. 1). Patch A is the background. Patch B will become the stripe, and Patch C will become the corner triangle. We will be using the corner-square method for sewing the block.

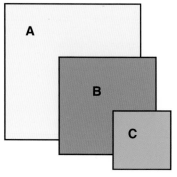
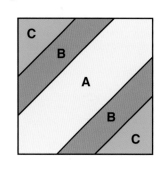

Fig. 1. Connector block squares

1. Draw a straight line from corner to corner on the wrong side of the B square, as shown in figure 2.

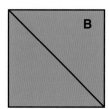

Fig. 2. Draw a diagonal line.

2. Lay square B on top of square A, right sides together and pin (fig. 3).

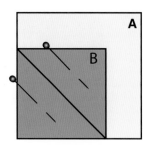

Fig. 3. Pin square B in place.

3. Because a fold in the fabric takes up space, you need to make allowance for that—do not sew on the line. Instead, sew a thread or two beyond the line, toward the corner of the square (fig. 4).

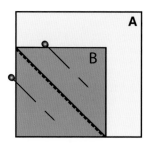

Fig. 4. Sew outside the line.

4. To check the accuracy of your seam, press B open, as shown in figure 5. The raw edges of B should align with those of A. If they do not, refer to Fixing the Seam on page 41.

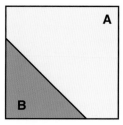

Fig. 5. Raw edges should align.

5. Use a rotary cutter and ruler to trim both A and B ¼" away from the sewn line (fig. 6). Press B open again.

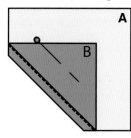

Fig. 6. Trim off the extra fabric.

6. Repeat steps 1–5 to add the C square to the A/B unit (fig. 7).

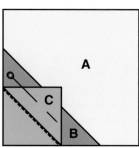

Fig. 7. Add C in the same way.

7. Use the same method to add B and C to the opposite corner of A, completing the Connector block (fig. 4–8).

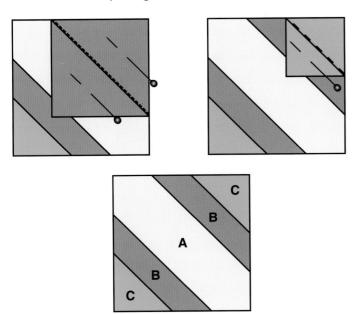

Fig. 8. Completed Connector block

Keeping Track
Before working on each block, check the block drawing for color placement. After you have made one Connector block, you can use it as a guide for making the rest in that color arrangement. This will help you make sure you are using the colors in the right places. It may also help to separate like blocks into stacks.

Fixing the Seam
If the edges of squares A and B do not align when you check your seam, look for the following problems: Did you draw the line accurately? Did the smaller square slip when you were sewing? Did you sew on the line rather than right next to it? Once you have determined what went wrong, you can remove the stitches and try again.

Nine-Patch Block

It's a good idea to sew one block and check your measurements. Once you are sure you are getting accurate results, you can stack the pieces for all like

blocks to the left of your sewing machine and sew them together assembly-line style.

1. Lay out the patches for one block. Sew the patches into rows then sew the rows together. Press the seam allowances as shown by the arrows in figure 4–9.

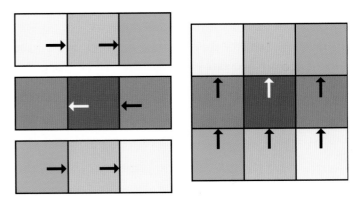

Fig. 9. Sewing sequence

2. As each block is finished, mist it with sizing and press. This step prevents the block from stretching and makes it perfectly flat.

3. Check the size of the block with a square ruler. The Nine-Patch block should be exactly the same size as your Connector blocks.

4. Follow your block chart to make the number of Nine-Patch blocks needed for your quilt.

Pinning for a Perfect Match
Here's my method for matching seams: On the pieces to be joined, make sure the seam allowances are pressed in opposite directions. Pin diagonally across the butted seams and pin the corners vertically (fig. 4–10). The diagonal pins will keep the seam lines from slipping as you sew.

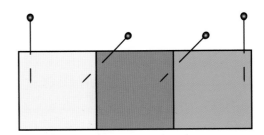

Fig. 10. Pinning to match seams

Pressing Options

Toward the dark. Pressing seam allowances toward the darker fabric is the traditional method. It is the fastest and simplest way to press. The seams are strong and keep the batting from creeping out along the seam lines. This method also keeps seam allowances from showing through the lighter fabric.

To press toward the dark, use the edge of your iron to push the seam allowances toward the darker fabric. (Lift most of the weight of the iron off the ironing surface as you push the allowances.) After the allowances have been pressed to one side, rest the full weight of the iron on the allowances as you press them again. Use a shot of sizing if desired.

Pressing open. This method requires more time and effort; however, the results are worth it. Open seam allowances produce a smooth quilt top that lies flat and hangs straight. It makes matching seams a snap. Today's modern battings are less likely to creep through the seams.

To press seam allowances open, smooth them open with your fingers. (If you find it difficult to open them, spray lightly with water. Let the piece set a minute as the water sinks into the fabric.) Rest the whole iron on the seam and give it a bit of sizing, if desired. Lift the iron straight up and repeat on the next seam.

Joining Blocks

Let me show you a simple way to match Nine-Patch to Connector blocks:

1. Using a sharp pencil and a ruler, mark the ¼" sewing line on the seam lines of the Connector and Nine-Patch blocks as shown in figure 11.

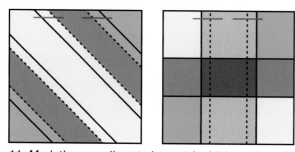

Fig. 11. Mark the seam lines to be matched (shown in red).

2. Place the blocks right sides together and match the pencil marks. Pin through the seam line and the marks on both blocks (fig. 12).

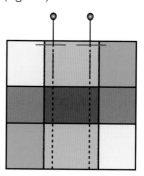

Fig. 12. First pinning

3. Leave this first pin in the seam and place a pin on either side of it. Then remove the center pin (fig. 13).

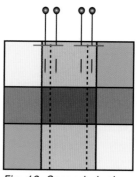

Fig. 13. Second pinning

Quilt Assembly

These blocks are easy to sew together. We are letting the color and the rotation of the blocks do all the work.

1. Lay out the blocks, making sure you have them all going in the correct direction. Double and triple check your layout with your drawing or the quilt pattern. It helps to walk away and look at the arrangement from across the room because mistakes are easier to see from a distance.

2. After checking your blocks, sew them into rows. Check the rows with your drawing one more time.

3. To make sure the seams will butt together easily, press one row to the right. Press the next row to the left. Continue alternating the pressing of the rows. Then join the rows.

Checking rows. Place a label at the same end of every row. This will keep your rows oriented correctly because you know those labels should line up. Another trick is to piece one fourth of the quilt design at a time. This makes it easier to spot mistakes.

Quilting Ideas

You have several options for quilting. You can outline quilt the Celtic bars and stipple quilt the open areas. However, the sky is the limit. Here are four whole-quilt quilting patterns to inspire you.

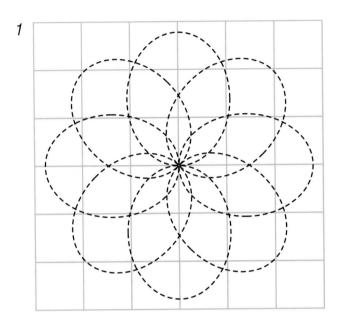

1

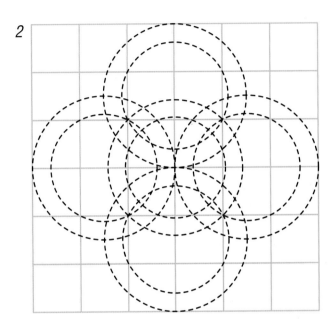

2

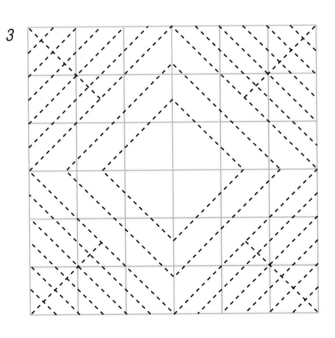

3

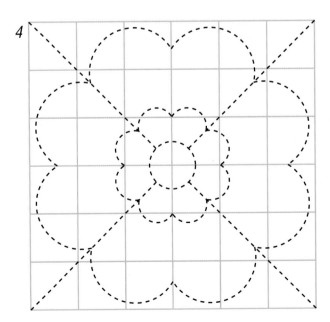

4

Chapter 5

Patch Patterns

Making Templates
Using Templates
Block Patterns

Some quilters prefer to use templates rather than rotary cut their patches. To use templates, follow these steps:

Making Templates

1. Place tracing paper over the desired patch pattern. Using a ruler and a pencil, trace the sewing and cutting lines and the grain line. Write the block size on the traced template. Using paper scissors, rough-cut the tracing-paper template, a bit larger than needed.

2. Smear glue from a glue stick onto template plastic and place the paper template on top of the glue. Smooth out any air bubbles and apply more glue to the edges, if needed.

3. Using paper scissors, cut the plastic template on the traced cutting line.

Using Templates

1. Place a single layer of fabric, wrong side up, on your cutting board.

2. Place the template, also wrong side up, on the fabric, making sure to align the grain line on the template with the lengthwise or crosswise fabric grain.

3. Using a sharp lead pencil, trace around the template. You can use a silver, white, or yellow pencil if you like. Trace around the template to make as many patches as you need, but mark on only half the width of the fabric.

4. Fold the fabric in half, with the template tracings face up. Make sure the fabric is not wrinkled. In the middle of each template, place a pin through both fabric layers.

5. Using your fabric scissors, cut the fabric pieces. If your scissors are sharp, you can have up to four to six layers of fabric. When cutting many layers, keep your scissors perpendicular to the fabric to ensure an accurate cut of all layers.

Patterns may be copied for personal use only.

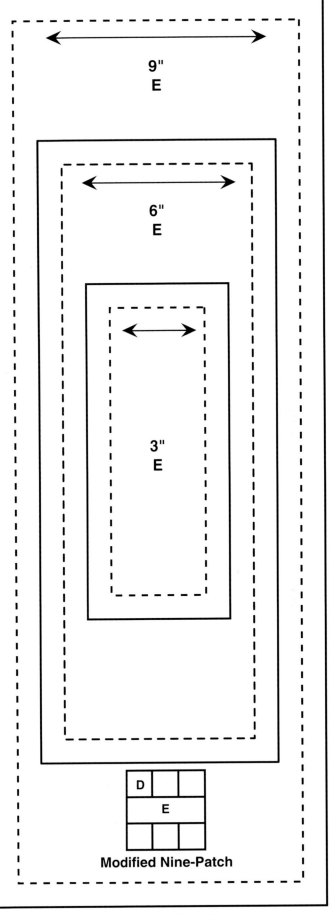

Patterns for Nine-Patch

Patch Patterns

Pattern for 3" finished blocks

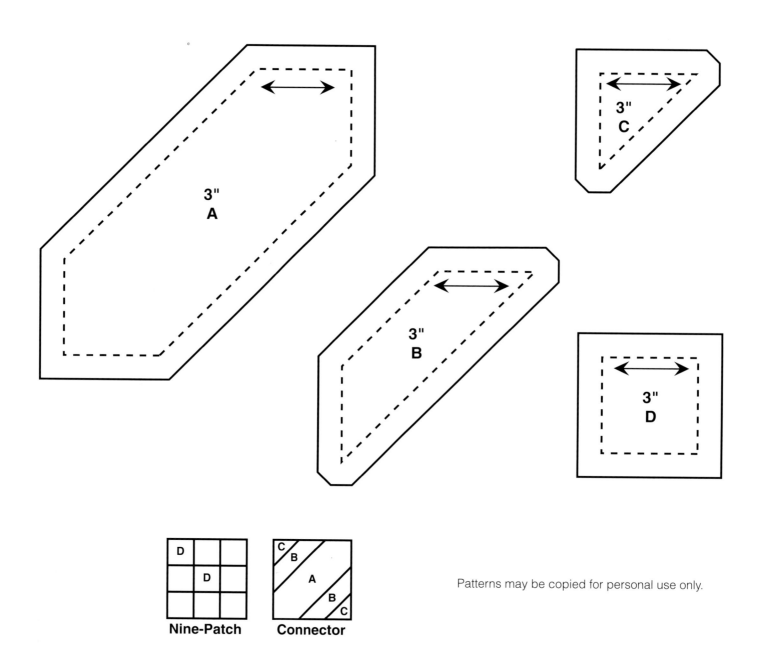

Patterns may be copied for personal use only.

Pattern for 6" finished blocks

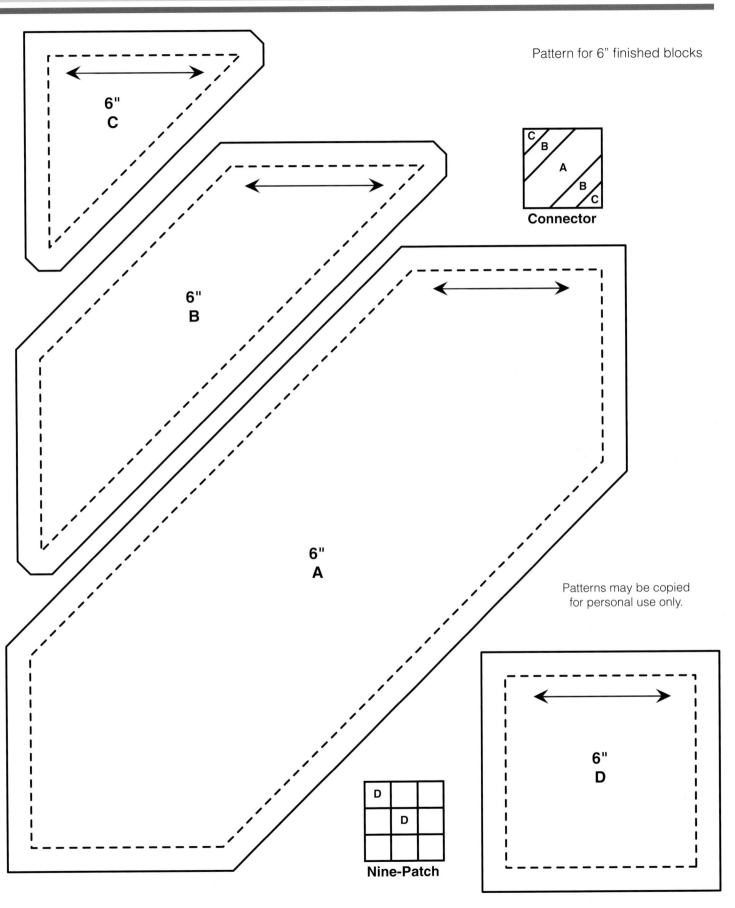

6"
C

6"
B

6"
A

Connector

Patterns may be copied
for personal use only.

6"
D

Nine-Patch

Patch Patterns

Pattern for 9" finished blocks

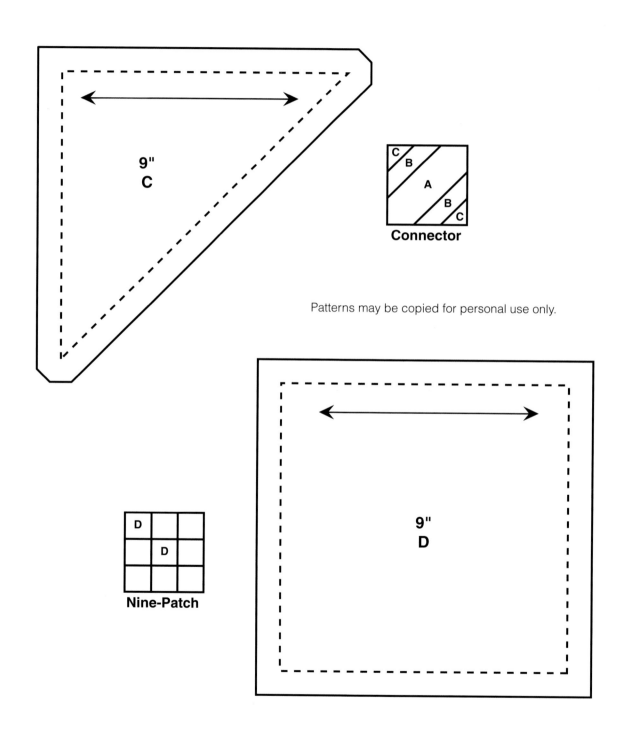

9"
C

Connector

Patterns may be copied for personal use only.

Nine-Patch

9"
D

Pattern for 9" finished blocks

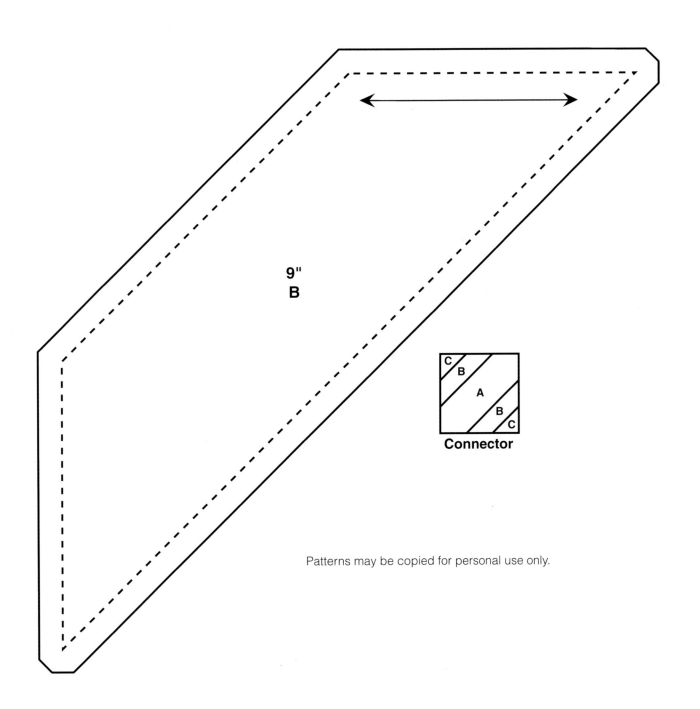

9"
B

Connector

Patterns may be copied for personal use only.

Patterns for 9" finished blocks

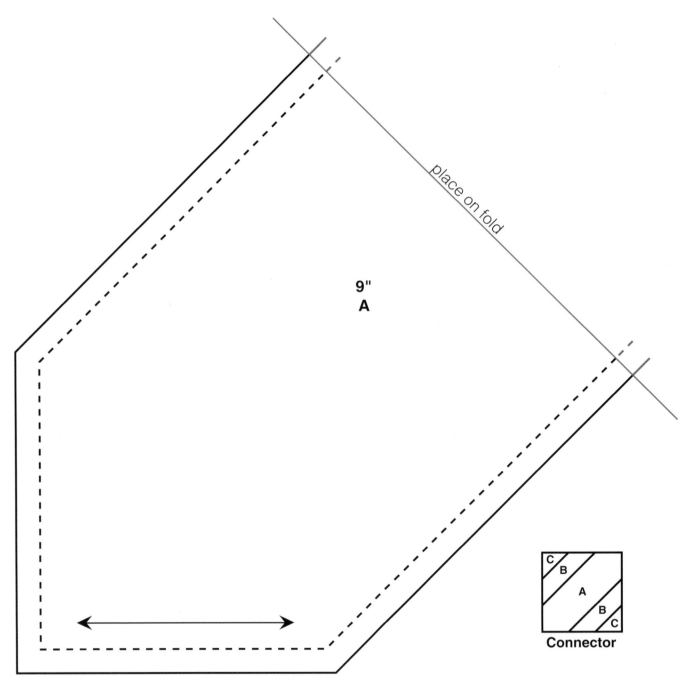

place on fold

9"
A

Connector

Patterns may be copied for personal use only.

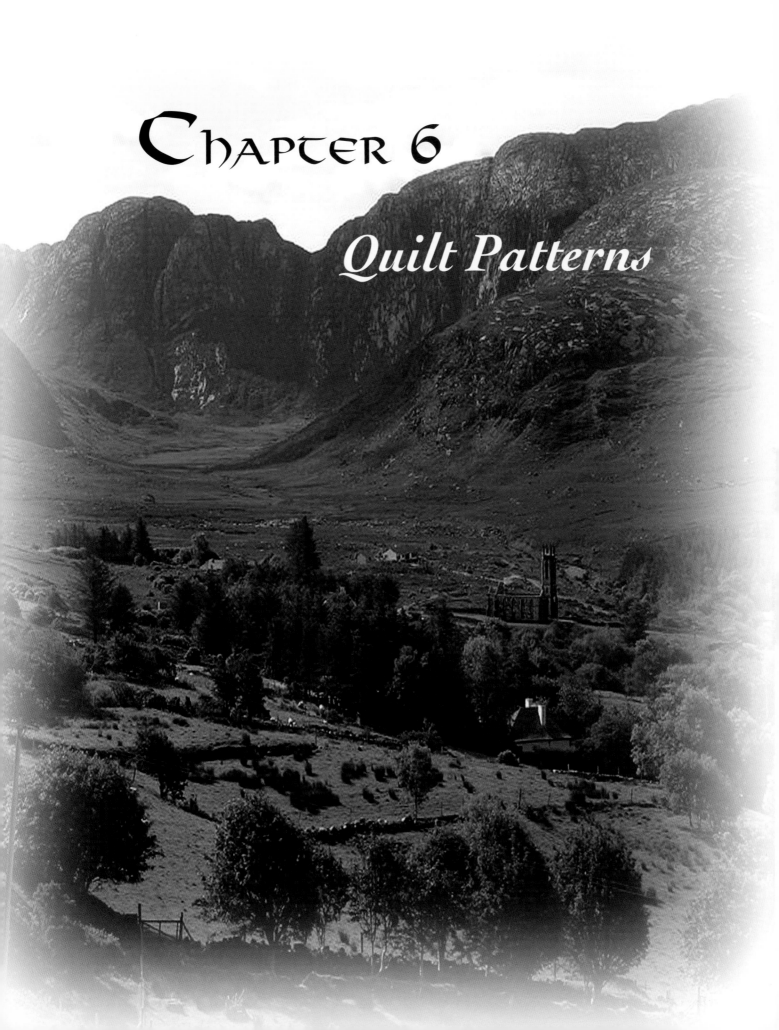

CHAPTER 6

Quilt Patterns

Celtic Charm

Finished quilt top: 36" x 36"

Designed by Lisa Newcomer, Frederick, Maryland;
made by the author; and quilted by Terry Dramstad, Cooperstown, North Dakota

Skill level: beginner
Finished block: 6"

Yardage & Cutting

Use fabric at least 40" wide. Cut strips selvage to selvage.

Fabric	First Cut	Second Cut
Cream 1¾ yd.		
Connector A	5 strips 6½"	28 squares 6½"
Nine-Patch & Connector C	5 strips 2½"	68 squares 2½"
Binding	4 strips 2"	(sew strips end to end)
Rust ¾ yd.		
Nine-Patch	2 strips 2½"	8 squares 2½" 4 rectangles 2½" x 6½"
Connector B	4 strips 4½"	28 squares 4½"
Medium Green ⅓ yd.		
Nine-Patch	1 strip 2½"	4 squares 2½" 2 rectangles 2½" x 6½"
Connector B	1 strip 4½"	4 squares 4½"
Dark Green ⅓ yd.		
Nine-Patch	1 strip 2½"	4 squares 2½" 2 rectangles 2½" x 6½"
Connector B	1 strip 4½"	4 squares 4½"
Backing 1¼ yd., 1 panel 40" x 40"		
Batting 40" x 40"		

Block Assembly

Connector Blocks

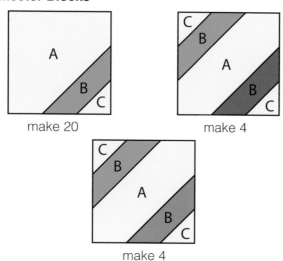

make 20

make 4

make 4

Nine-Patch Blocks

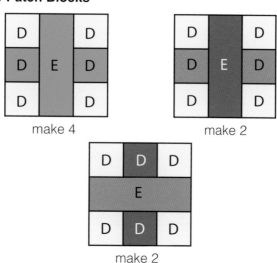

make 4

make 2

make 2

1. Paying close attention to color placement, make all the blocks shown in the block assembly diagrams. (Block assembly instructions begin on page 40.)

2. Spray the blocks with sizing and press. The sewn blocks should measure 6½" square.

Quilt Assembly
Reflections and Rotation

1. To make it easier to arrange the blocks and see that they are positioned correctly, lay out and sew a quarter of the design at a time. Then sew the quarters together to complete the quilt top.

Quarter quilt assembly

2. Layer the quilt top with batting and backing; baste. Quilt the layers (see quilting ideas on page 43). Bind the raw edges and label your quilt.

Quilt assembly

Celtic Vision

Finished quilt top: 42" x 42"

Designed and made by Ellen White, Jackson, Georgia

Skill level: beginner
Finished block: 6"

Yardage & Cutting

Use fabric at least 40" wide. Cut strips selvage to selvage, except borders.

Fabric	First Cut	Second Cut
Cream ¾ yd.		
Connector A	3 strips 6½"	16 squares 6½"
Nine-Patch	1 strip 2½"	8 squares 2½"
Navy ¾ yd.		
Nine-Patch Connector C	3 strips 2½"	12 squares 2½" 12 rectangles 2½" x 6½"
Connector B	3 strips 4½"	24 squares 4½"
Rust 1 yd.		
Connector A	1 strip 6½"	4 squares 6½"
Nine-Patch Connector C	6 strips 2½"	52 squares 2½" 16 rectangles 2½" x 6½"
Connector B	1 strip 4½"	8 squares 4½"
Orange 2 yd.		
Border	(cut strips parallel to selvages)	4 strips 3½" x 44½"
Nine-Patch	2 strips 2½"	8 squares 2½" 4 rectangles 2½" x 6½"
Connector B	1 strip 4½"	4 squares 4½"
Binding	5 strips 2"	(sew strips end to end)
Backing 2⅞ yd., 2 panels 25" x 48"		
Batting 48" x 48"		

Block Assembly

Connector Blocks

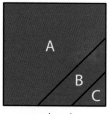

make 4

make 8

make 8

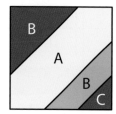

make 4

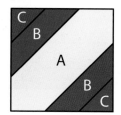

make 4

Nine-Patch Blocks

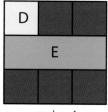

make 4

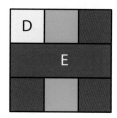

make 4

1. Paying close attention to color placement, make all the blocks shown in the block assembly diagrams. (Block assembly instructions begin on page 40.)

2. Spray the blocks with sizing and press. The sewn blocks should measure 6½" square.

Quilt Assembly

Rotation

1. To make it easier to arrange the blocks and see that they are positioned correctly, lay out and sew a quarter of the design at a time. Then sew the quarters together to complete the quilt top.

2. Sew the border strips to the quilt top and miter the corners.

3. Sew the two backing panels together on one long side. Press the seam allowances open.

4. Layer the quilt top with batting and backing; baste. Quilt the layers (see quilting ideas on page 43). Bind the raw edges and label your quilt.

Quarter quilt, make 4

Quilt assembly

Celtic *Cross*

Finished quilt top: 48" x 48"

Designed by Lyn Anderson, Rooseveltown, New York;
made by the author; and quilted by Terry Dramstad, Cooperstown, North Dakota

Skill level: beginner
Finished block: 6"

Yardage & Cutting

Use fabric at least 40" wide. Cut strips selvage to selvage.

Fabric	First Cut	Second Cut
Blue ⅔ yd.		
Connector A	1 strip 6½"	4 squares 6½"
Nine-Patch Connector C	5 strips 2½"	56 squares 2½" 8 rectangles 2½" x 6½"
Black 1¼ yd.		
Connector B	5 strips 4½"	40 squares 4½"
Nine-Patch	6 strips 2½"	24 squares 2½" 24 rectangles 2½" x 6½"
Beige 2 yd.		
Connector A	6 strips 6½"	36 squares 6½"
Nine-Patch Connector C	5 strips 2½"	32 squares 2½" 16 rectangles 2½" x 6½"
Binding	6 strips 2"	(sew strips end to end)

Backing 3¼ yd., 2 panels 28" x 54"

Batting 54" x 54"

Block Assembly

Plain Blocks

make 12

Connector Blocks

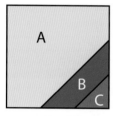

make 16

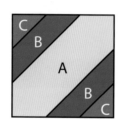

make 8

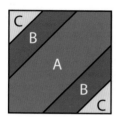

make 4

Nine-Patch Blocks

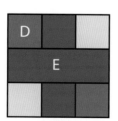

make 4

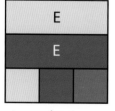

make 8

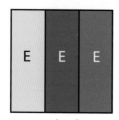

make 4

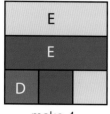

make 8

1. Paying close attention to color placement, make all the blocks shown in the block assembly diagrams. (Block assembly instructions begin on page 40.)

2. Spray the blocks with sizing and press. The sewn blocks should measure 6½" square.

Quilt Assembly
Rotation

1. To make it easier to arrange the blocks and see that they are positioned correctly, lay out and sew one-fourth of the design at a time. Then sew the quarters together to complete the quilt top.

2. Sew the two backing panels together on one long side. Press the seam allowances open.

3. Layer the quilt top with batting and backing; baste. Quilt the layers (see quilting ideas on page 43). Bind the raw edges and label your quilt.

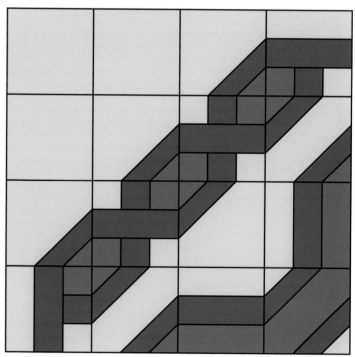

Quarter quilt, make 4

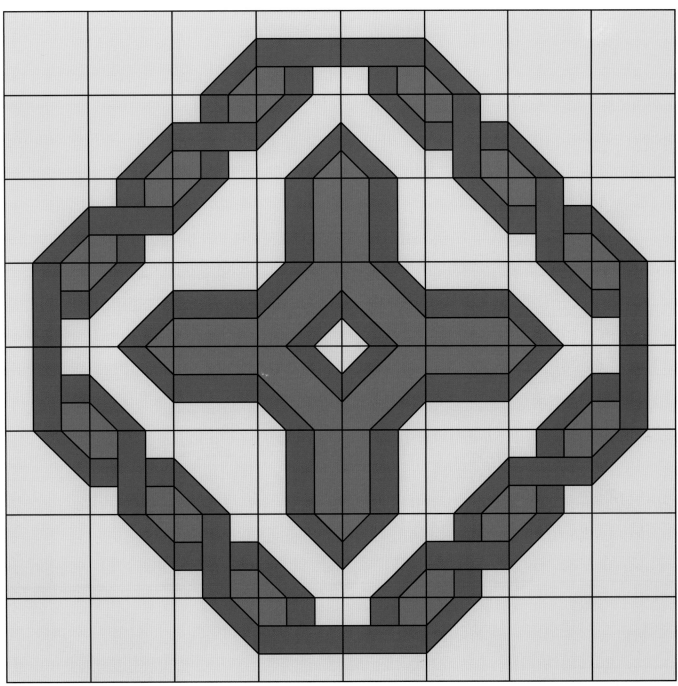

Quilt assembly

Celtic Roundabout

Finished quilt top: 48" x 48"

Designed and made by the author;
quilted by Terry Dramstad, Cooperstown, North Dakota

Skill level: beginner
Finished block: 6"

Yardage & Cutting

Use fabric at least 40" wide. Cut strips selvage to selvage.

Fabric	First Cut	Second Cut
Peach 2½ yd.		
Connector A	7 strips 6½"	40 squares 6½"
Nine-Patch Connector C	10 strips 2½"	156 squares 2½"
Binding	5 strips 2"	(sew strips end to end)
Medium Green 1 yd.		
Connector B	4 strips 4½"	32 squares 4½"
Nine-Patch	4 strips 2½"	64 squares 2½"
Dark Green ¼ yd.		
Nine-Patch	1 strip 2½"	16 squares 2½"
Medium Blue ¾ yd.		
Connector B	4 strips 4½"	28 squares 4½"
Nine-Patch	2 strips 2½"	32 squares 2½"
Dark Blue ¼ yd.		
Nine-Patch	1 strip 2½"	8 squares 2½"

Backing 3¼ yd., 2 panels 27" x 54"

Batting 54" x 54"

Block Assembly

Connector Blocks

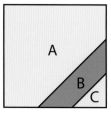

make 12

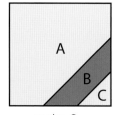

make 8

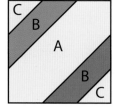

make 20

Nine-Patch Blocks

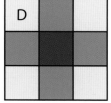

make 8

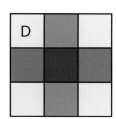

make 8

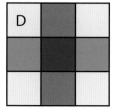

make 8

1. Paying close attention to color placement, make all the blocks shown in the block assembly diagrams.

2. Spray the blocks with sizing and press. The sewn blocks should measure 6½" square. (Block assembly instructions begin on page 40.)

Quilt Assembly

Rotation

1. To make it easier to arrange the blocks and see that they are positioned correctly, lay out and sew a quarter of the design at a time. Then sew the quarters together to complete the quilt top.

2. Sew the panels together on one long side. Press the seam allowances open.

3. Layer the quilt top with batting and backing; baste. Quilt the layers (see quilting ideas on page 43). Bind the raw edges and label your quilt.

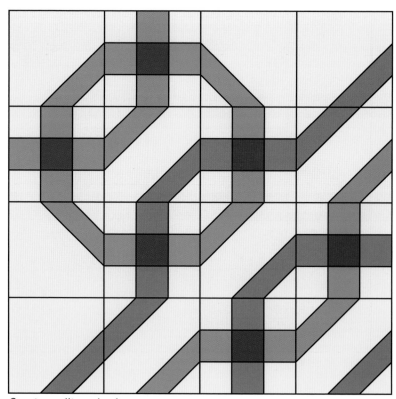

Quarter quilt, make 4

Quilt assembly

Celtic Reflections

Finished quilt top: 36" x 36"

Designed and made by the author;
quilted by Terry Dramstad, Cooperstown, North Dakota

Skill level: beginner
Finished block: 3"

Yardage & Cutting

Use fabric at least 40" wide. Cut strips selvage to selvage.

Fabric	First Cut	Second Cut
Light Teal 1¾ yd.		
Connector A Plain Blocks	9 strips 3½"	96 squares 3½"
Nine-Patch Connector C	13 strips 1½"	324 squares 1½"
Binding	4 strips 2"	(sew strips end to end)
Medium Blue ⅝ yd.		
Connector B	4 strips 2½"	64 squares 2½"
Nine-Patch	4 strips 1½"	96 squares 1½"
Dark Blue ⅛ yd.		
Nine-Patch	1 strip 1½"	24 squares 1½"
Medium Green ⅝ yd.		
Connector B	5 strips 2½"	68 squares 2½"
Nine-Patch	4 strips 1½"	96 squares 1½"
Dark Green ⅛ yd.		
Nine-Patch	1 strip 2½"	24 squares 1½"

Backing 1¼ yd., 1 panel 40" x 40"

Batting 40" x 40"

Block Assembly

Plain Blocks

make 12

Connector Blocks

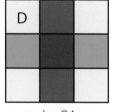

make 16

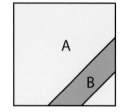

make 20

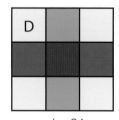

make 48

Nine-Patch Blocks

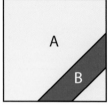

make 24

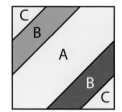

make 24

1. Paying close attention to color placement, make all the blocks shown in the block assembly diagram.

2. Spray the blocks with sizing and press. The sewn blocks should measure 3½" square. (Block assembly instructions begin on page 40.)

Quilt Assembly

Rotation

1. To make it easier to arrange the blocks and see that they are positioned correctly, lay out and sew one-fourth of the design at a time. Then sew the quarters together to complete the quilt top.

2. Sew the two backing panels together on one long side. Press the seam allowances open.

3. Layer the quilt top with batting and backing; baste. Quilt the layers (see quilting ideas on page 43). Bind the raw edges and label your quilt.

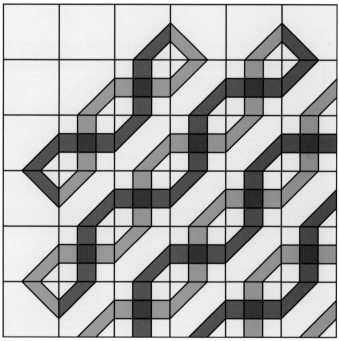

Quarter quilt, make 4

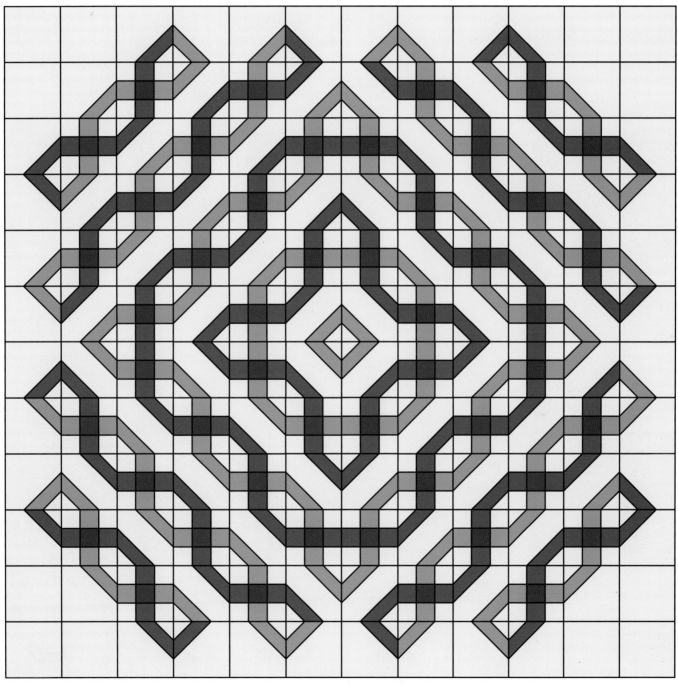

Quilt assembly

Celtic *Fire*

Finished quilt top: 24" x 24"

Designed and made by the author;
quilted by Terry Dramstad, Cooperstown, North Dakota

Skill level: intermediate
Finished block: 3"

Yardage & Cutting

Use fabric at least 40" wide. Cut strips selvage to selvage.

Fabric	First Cut	Second Cut
Black 1¼ yd.		
Connector A	6 strips 3½"	56 squares 3½"
Nine-Patch Connector C	6 strips 1½"	144 squares 1½"
Binding	3 strips 2"	(sew strips end to end)
Purple ⅓ yd.		
Connector B	3 strips 2½"	48 squares 2½"
Red-Violet ⅓ yd.		
Connector B	1 strip 2½"	12 squares 2½"
Nine-Patch	1 strip 1½"	16 squares 1½"
Gold ⅓ yd.		
Connector B	3 strips 2½"	48 squares 2½"
Medium Green ¼ yd.		
Connector B	1 strip 2½"	4 squares 2½"
Nine-Patch	1 strip 1½"	8 squares 1½" 4 rectangles 1½" x 3½"
Dark Green ¼ yd.		
Nine-Patch	1 strip 1½"	4 squares 1½"

Backing ⅞ yd., 1 panel 28" x 28"

Batting 28" x 28"

Fire

Block Assembly

Connector Blocks

make 4

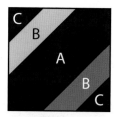

make 24

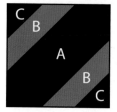

make 12

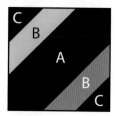

make 12

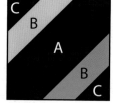

make 4

Nine-Patch Blocks

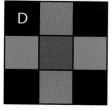

make 4

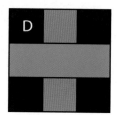

make 4

1. Paying close attention to color placement, make all the blocks shown in the block assembly diagrams.

2. Spray the blocks with sizing and press. The sewn blocks should measure 3½" square. (Block assembly instructions begin on page 40.)

Quilt Assembly

Rotation

1. To make it easier to arrange the blocks and see that they are positioned correctly, lay out and sew a quarter of the design at a time. Then sew the quarters together to complete the quilt top.

2. Layer the quilt top with batting and backing; baste. Quilt the layers (see quilting ideas on page 43). Bind the raw edges and label your quilt.

Quarter quilt, make 4

Quilt assembly

Celtic Hearts

Finished quilt top: 24" x 24"

Designed and made by the author;
quilted by Terry Dramstad, Cooperstown, North Dakota

Skill level: intermediate
Finished block: 3"

Yardage & Cutting

Use fabric at least 40" wide. Cut strips selvage to selvage.

Fabric	First Cut	Second Cut
Light Purple ⅝ yd.		
Connector A	2 strips 3½"	16 squares 3½"
Nine-Patch Connector C	5 strips 1½"	96 squares 1½" 8 rectangles 1½" x 3½"
Medium Purple ⅝ yd.		
Connector A	4 strips 3½"	36 squares 3½"
Nine-Patch Connector C	2 strips 1½"	40 squares 1½"
Dark Purple ⅝ yd.		
Connector B	3 strips 2½"	40 squares 2½"
Nine-Patch	1 strip 1½"	24 squares 1½"
Binding	3 strips 2"	(sew strips end to end)
Red ¼ yd.		
Connector B	2 strips 2½"	28 squares 2½"
Nine-Patch	1 strip 1½"	4 squares 1½" 2 rectangles 1½" x 3½"
Pink ¼ yd.		
Connector B	2 strips 2½"	28 squares 2½"
Nine-Patch	1 strip 1½"	4 squares 1½" 2 rectangles 1½" x 3½"

Backing ⅞ yd., 1 panel 28" x 28"

Batting 28" x 28"

Block Assembly

Connector Blocks

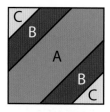

make 8

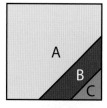

make 8

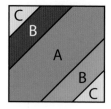

make 8

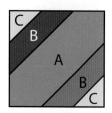

make 8

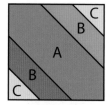

make 12

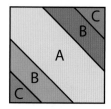

make 8

Nine-Patch Blocks

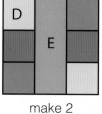

make 2

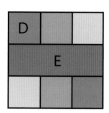

make 2

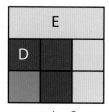

make 8

1. Paying close attention to color placement, make all the blocks shown in the block assembly diagrams.

2. Spray the blocks with sizing and press. The sewn blocks should measure 3½" square. (Block assembly instructions begin on page 40.)

Quilt Assembly

Reflection

1. To make it easier to arrange the blocks and see that they are positioned correctly, lay out and sew a quarter of the design at a time. Note that the quarter quilts are mirror images.

2. Being careful to position the quarters correctly, sew them together to complete the quilt top.

3. Layer the quilt top with batting and backing; baste. Quilt the layers (see quilting ideas on page 43). Bind the raw edges and label your quilt.

Quarter quilt, make 2

Quarter quilt, make 2

Quilt assembly

Quest

Finished quilt top: 51" x 51"

Designed and made by the author;
quilted by Terry Dramstad, Cooperstown, North Dakota

Skill level: intermediate
Finished block: 6"

Yardage & Cutting

Use fabric at least 40" wide. Cut strips selvage to selvage.

Fabric	First Cut	Second Cut
Cream 2 yds.		
Connector A	7 strips 6½"	40 squares 6½"
Nine-Patch Connector C	7 strips 2½"	104 squares 2½"
Tan 1 yd.		
Connector A	1 strip 6½"	4 squares 6½"
Nine-Patch Connector C	2 strips 2½"	28 squares 2½"
Side triangles	2 strips 9¾"	6 squares 9¾ (cut diagonally twice to make 24 quarter-square triangles)
Medium Green 1¼ yds.		
Connector B	4 strips 4½"	32 squares 4½"
Nine-Patch	2 strips 2½"	8 squares 2½" 4 rectangles 2½" x 6½"
Binding	6 strips 2"	(sew strips end to end)
Red ⅝ yd.		
Connector B	2 strips 4½"	16 squares 4½"
Nine-Patch	3 strips 2½"	16 squares 2½" 8 rectangles 2½" x 6½"
Blue ⅝ yd.		
Connector B	3 strips 4½"	20 squares 4½"
Nine-Patch	2 strips 2½"	8 squares 2½" 4 rectangles 2½" x 6½"

Backing 3½ yds., cut 2 panels 31" x 59"

Batting 59" x 59"

Block Assembly

Connector Blocks

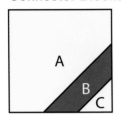
make 16

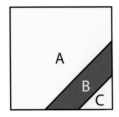
make 4

make 8

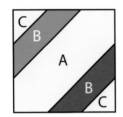
make 8

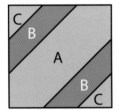
make 4

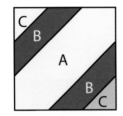
make 4

Nine-Patch Blocks

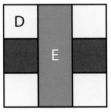
make 4

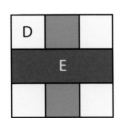
make 4

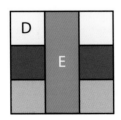
make 4

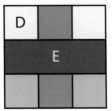
make 4

1. Paying close attention to color placement, make all the blocks shown in the block assembly diagrams.

2. Spray the blocks with sizing and press. The sewn blocks should measure 6½" square. (Block assembly instructions begin on page 40.)

Quilt Assembly

Rotation
Assemble in diagonal rows.

1. Arrange the blocks and side triangles as shown. Sew the blocks and triangles into diagonal rows then sew the rows together to complete the quilt top.

2. Sew the two backing panels together on one long side. Press the seam allowances open.

3. Layer the quilt top with batting and backing; baste. Quilt the layers (see quilting ideas on page 43). Bind the raw edges and label your quilt.

Quilt assembly

Celtic Rose Window

Finished quilt top: 48" x 48"

Designed and made by the author;
quilted by Terry Dramstad, Cooperstown, North Dakota

Skill level: intermediate
Finished block: 6"

Yardage & Cutting

Use fabric at least 40" wide. Cut strips selvage to selvage.

Fabric	First Cut	Second Cut
Light Blue 1½ yd.		
Connector A	4 strips 6½"	20 squares 6½"
Nine-Patch	3 strips 2½"	12 squares 2½" 8 rectangles 2½" x 6½"
Binding	6 strips 2"	(sew strips end to end)
Medium Blue ¾ yd.		
Connector A	2 strips 6½"	8 squares 6½"
Nine-Patch & Connector C	4 strips 2½"	64 squares 2½"
Dark blue ¾ yd.		
Connector A	2 strips 6½"	12 squares 6½"
Nine-Patch Connector C	4 strips 2½"	60 squares 2½"
Gold 1⅝ yd.		
Connector B	7 strips 4½"	56 squares 4½"
Nine-Patch	6 strips 2½"	88 squares 2½"
Orange ¼ yd.		
Nine-Patch	2 strips 2½"	24 squares 2½"

Backing 3¼ yds., 2 panels 28" x 54"

Batting 54" x 54"

Block Assembly

Plain Blocks

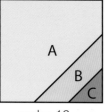

make 4

Connector Blocks

make 16

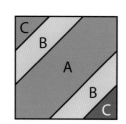

make 8

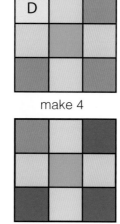

make 12

Nine-Patch Blocks

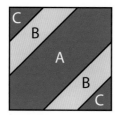

make 8

make 4

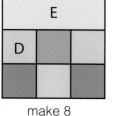

make 4

make 4

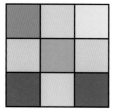

make 4

1. Paying close attention to color placement, make all the blocks shown in the block assembly diagrams.

2. Spray the blocks with sizing and press. The sewn blocks should measure 6½" square. (Block assembly instructions begin on page 40.)

Quilt Assembly

Rotation

1. To make it easier to arrange the blocks and see that they are positioned correctly, lay out and sew a quarter of the design at a time. Then sew the quarters together to complete the quilt top.

2. Layer the quilt top with batting and backing; baste. Quilt the layers (see quilting ideas on page 43). Bind the raw edges and label your quilt.

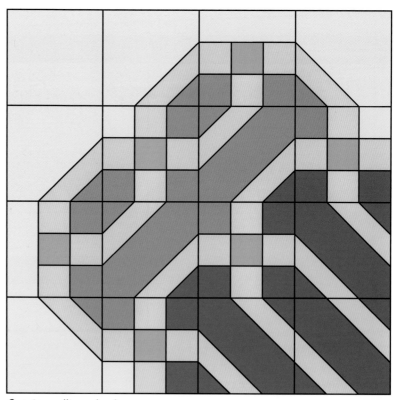

Quarter quilt, make 4

Quilt assembly

Celtic *Rings*

Finished quilt top: 48" x 48"

Designed, made, and quilted by the author

Skill level: intermediate
Finished block: 6"

Yardage & Cutting

Use fabric at least 40" wide. Cut strips selvage to selvage.

Fabric	First Cut	Second Cut
Light Green 1 yd.		
Connector A	2 strips 6½"	8 squares 6½"
Nine-Patch & Connector C	3 strips 2½"	32 squares 2½"
Binding	6 strips 2"	(sew strips end to end)
Medium Green 1½ yd.		
Connector A	5 strips 6½"	28 squares 6½"
Nine-Patch & Connector C	5 strips 2½"	72 squares 2½"
Gold ⅝ yd.		
Connector A	2 strips 6½"	12 squares 6½"
Nine-Patch Connector C	2 strips 2½"	24 squares 2½"
Medium Blue ¾ yd.		
Connector B	4 strips 4½"	28 squares 4½"
Nine-Patch	2 strips 2½"	32 squares 2½"
Dark Blue ⅛ yd.		
Nine-Patch	1 strip 2½"	8 squares 2½"
Medium Purple ⅞ yd.		
Connector B	5 strips 4½"	36 squares 4½"
Nine-Patch	2 strips 2½"	32 squares 2½"
Dark Purple ⅛ yd.		
Nine-Patch	1 strip 2½"	8 squares 2½"

Backing 3¼ yd., 2 panels 28" x 54"

Batting 54" x 54"

Block Assembly

Plain Blocks

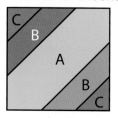

make 4

Connector Blocks

make 8

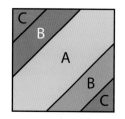

make 12

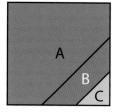

make 16

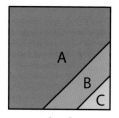

make 8

Nine-Patch Blocks

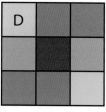

make 8

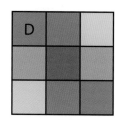

make 8

1. Paying close attention to color placement, make all the blocks shown in the block assembly diagrams.

2. Spray the blocks with sizing and press. The sewn blocks should measure 6½" square. (Block assembly instructions begin on page 40.)

Quilt Assembly

Rotation

1. To make it easier to arrange the blocks and see that they are positioned correctly, lay out and sew a quarter of the design at a time. Then sew the quarters together to complete the quilt top.

2. Layer the quilt top with batting and backing; baste. Quilt the layers (see quilting ideas on page 43). Bind the raw edges and label your quilt.

Quarter quilt, make 4

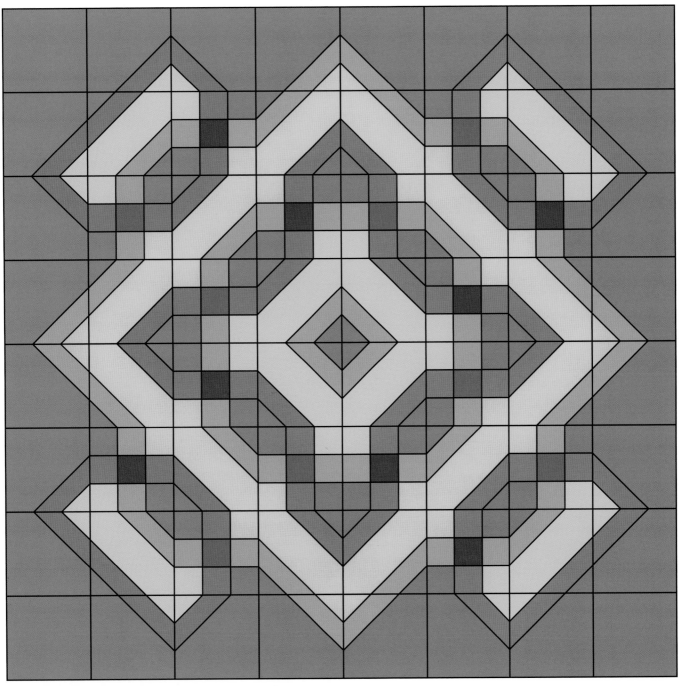

Quilt assembly

Celtic Lavender & Lace

Finished quilt top: 60" x 60"

Designed and made by the author;
quilted by Terry Dramstad, Cooperstown, North Dakota

Skill level: Advanced
Finished block: 6"

Yardage & Cutting

Use fabric at least 40" wide. Cut strips selvage to selvage.

Fabric	First Cut	Second Cut
Peach 1¾ yd.		
Connector A	5 strips 6½"	28 squares 6½"
Nine-Patch Connector C	2 strips 2½"	8 squares 2½" 8 rectangles 2½" x 6½"
Binding	7 strips 2"	(sew strips end to end)
Brown ⅞ yd.		
Connector A	3 strips 6½"	16 squares 6½"
Nine-Patch	2 strips 2½"	32 squares 2½"
Copper 1½ yd.		
Connector A	3 strips 6½"	16 squares 6½"
Nine-Patch Connector C	13 strips 2½"	176 squares 2½" 8 rectangles 2½" x 6½"
Light Purple 1 yd.		
Connector B	5 strips 4½"	36 squares 4½"
Nine-Patch	3 strips 2½"	16 squares 2½" 8 rectangles 2½" x 6½"
Dark Purple ⅜ yd.		
Connector B	1 strip 4½"	4 squares 4½"
Nine-Patch	2 strips 2½"	8 squares 2½" 4 rectangles 2½" x 6½"
Light Green ⅝ yd.		
Connector B	2 strips 4½"	16 squares 4½"
Nine-Patch	3 strips 2½"	8 squares 2½" 12 rectangles 2½" x 6½"
Medium Green ⅝ yd.		
Connector B	2 strips 4½"	16 squares 4½"
Nine-Patch	3 strips 2½"	16 squares 2½"
		8 rectangles 2½" x 6½"
Dark Green ⅝ yd.		
Connector B	2 strips 4½"	16 squares 4½"
Nine-Patch	3 strips 2½"	16 squares 2½" 8 rectangles 2½" x 6½"

Backing 4 yd., 2 panels 35" x 68"

Batting 68" x 68"

Block Assembly

Connector Blocks

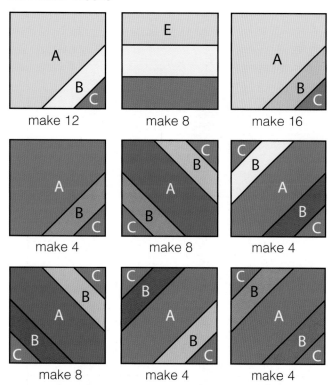

make 12   make 8   make 16

make 4   make 8   make 4

make 8   make 4   make 4

Nine-Patch Blocks

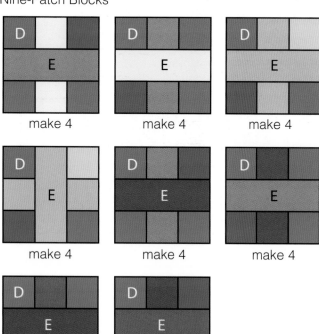

make 4   make 4   make 4

make 4   make 4   make 4

make 4   make 4

1. Paying close attention to color placement, make all the blocks shown in the block assembly diagrams.

2. Spray the blocks with sizing and press. The sewn blocks should measure 6½" square. (Block assembly instructions begin on page 40.)

Quilt Assembly

Rotation

1. To make it easier to arrange the blocks and see that they are positioned correctly, lay out and sew a quarter of the design at a time. Then sew the quarters together to complete the quilt top.

2. Layer the quilt top with batting and backing; baste. Quilt the layers (see quilting ideas on page 43). Bind the raw edges and label your quilt.

Quarter quilt, make 4

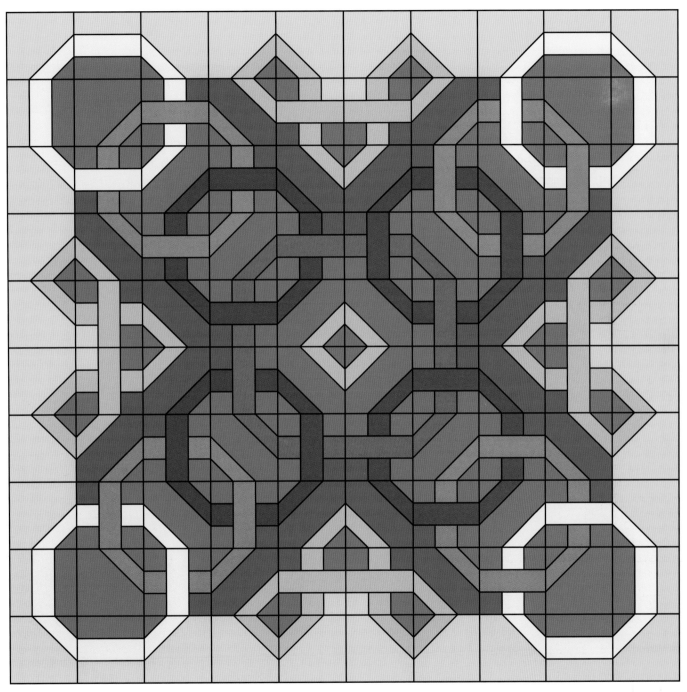

Quilt assembly

Celtic *Fantasy*

Finished quilt top: 60" x 60"

Designed and made by the author;
quilted by Terry Dramstad, Cooperstown, North Dakota

Skill level: Advanced
Finished block: 6"

Yardage & Cutting

Use fabric at least 40" wide. Cut strips selvage to selvage.

Fabric	First Cut	Second Cut
Light Pink 1¾ yd.		
Connector A	6 strips 6½"	36 squares 6½"
Connector C	2 strips 2½"	28 squares 2½"
Binding	7 strips 2"	(sew strips end to end)
Medium Pink ⅜ yd.		
Connector B	2 strips 4½"	12 squares 4½"
Dark Pink ¼ yd.		
Connector B	1 strip 4½"	4 squares 4½"
Multi-colored Print 1¼ yd.		
Connector A	3 strips 6½"	16 squares 6½"
Nine-Patch Connector C	5 strips 2½"	68 squares 2½"
Yellow ¾ yd.		
Connector B	5 strips 4½"	36 squares 4½"
Bronze ¾ yd.		
Connector B	4 strips 4½"	28 squares 4½"
Nine-Patch	1 strip 2½"	8 squares 2½"
Light Gray 1¾ yd.		
Connector A	6 strips 6½"	32 squares 6½"
Nine-Patch Connector C	7 strips 2½"	100 squares 2½"
Teal ⅜ yd.		
Connector B	2 strips 4½"	16 squares 4½"
Medium Blue 1⅛ yd.		
Connector B	5 strips 4½"	36 squares 4½"
Nine-Patch	4 strips 2½"	48 squares 2½" 4 rectangles 2½" x 6½"
Dark Blue ¼ yd.		
Nine-Patch	1 strip 2½"	12 squares 2½"

Backing 4 yd., 2 panels 35" x 68"

Batting 68" x 68"

Block Assembly

Connector Blocks

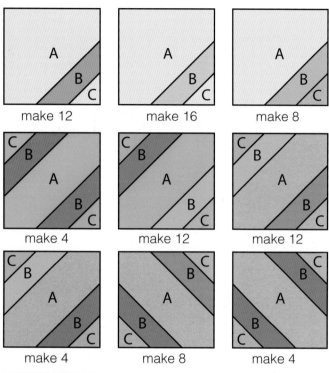

make 12   make 16   make 8

make 4   make 12   make 12

make 4   make 8   make 4

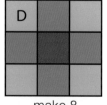

make 4

Nine-Patch Blocks

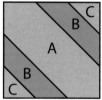

make 8   make 4

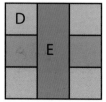

make 4

1. Paying close attention to color placement, make all the blocks shown in the block assembly diagrams.

2. Spray the blocks with sizing and press. The sewn blocks should measure 6½" square. (Block assembly instructions begin on page 40.)

Quilt Assembly

Reflections

1. To make it easier to arrange the blocks and see that they are positioned correctly, lay out and sew half of the design at a time. Then sew the halves together to complete the quilt top.

2. Layer the quilt top with batting and backing; baste. Quilt the layers (see quilting ideas on page 43). Bind the raw edges and label your quilt.

Half quilt, make 2

Quilt assembly

Celtic *Dawn*

Finished quilt top: 42" x 42"

Designed and made by the author;
quilted by Terry Dramstad, Cooperstown, North Dakota

Skill level: Advanced
Finished block: 3"

Yardage & Cutting

Use fabric at least 40" wide. Cut strips selvage to selvage.

Fabric	First Cut	Second Cut
Dark Rust 1 yd.		
Connector A	3 strips 3½"	32 squares 3½"
Nine-Patch Connector C	7 strips 1½"	172 squares 1½"
Binding	5 strips 2"	(sew strips end to end)
Dark Orange 1 yd.		
Connector A	4 strips 3½"	40 squares 3½"
Nine-Patch Connector C	9 strips 1½"	216 squares 1½"
Medium Orange ⅝ yd.		
Connector A	2 strips 3½"	16 squares 3½"
Nine Patch Connector C	5 strips 1½"	108 squares 1½"
Peach ⅝ yd.		
Connector A	2 strips 3½"	12 squares 3½"
Nine-Patch Connector C	4 strips 1½"	92 squares 1½"
Blue 1⅞ yd.		
Connector B	13 strips 2½"	196 squares 2½"
Nine-Patch	19 strips 1½"	472 squares 1½"

Backing 2⅞ yd. 2 panels 42" x 49"

Batting 48" x 48"

Block Assembly

Connector Blocks

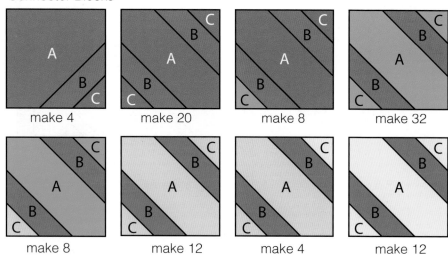

make 4   make 20   make 8   make 32

make 8   make 12   make 4   make 12

Nine-Patch Blocks

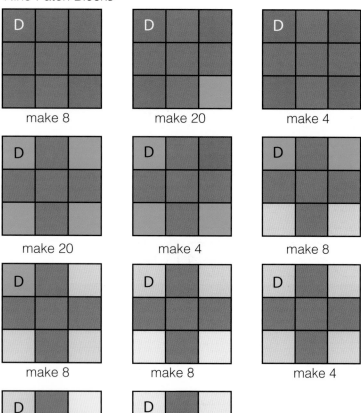

make 8   make 20   make 4

make 20   make 4   make 8

make 8   make 8   make 4

make 4   make 8

1. Paying close attention to color placement, make all the blocks shown in the block assembly diagrams.

2. Spray the blocks with sizing and press. The sewn blocks should measure 3½" square. (Block assembly instructions begin on page 40.)

Quilt Assembly

Rotation

1. To make it easier to arrange the blocks and see that they are positioned correctly, lay out and sew a half of the design at a time. Then sew the halves together to complete the quilt top.

2. Layer the quilt top with batting and backing; baste. Quilt the layers (see quilting ideas on page 43). Bind the raw edges and label your quilt.

Half quilt, make 2

Quilt assembly

Celtic *Maze*

Finished quilt top: 60" x 84"

Made by Sally Catlin, Ephrata, Washington

Skill level: Advanced
Finished block: 6"

Yardage & Cutting

Use fabric at least 40" wide. Cut strips selvage to selvage.

Fabric	First Cut	Second Cut
Light Blue 1 yd.		
Connector B	4 strips 4½"	32 squares 4½"
Nine-Patch	4 strips 2½"	32 squares 2½" 10 rectangles 2½" x 6½"
Medium Blue 4⅜ yd.		
Connector A	16 strips 6½"	88 squares 6½"
Nine-Patch & Connector C	10 strips 2½"	144 squares 2½" 4 rectangles 2½" x 6½"
Binding	8 strips 2"	(sew strips end to end)
Dark Blue ⅞ yd.		
Connector A	1 strip 6½"	4 squares 6½"
Nine Patch & Connector C	8 strips 2½"	124 squares 2½"
Light Pink 1 yd.		
Connector B	4 strips 4½"	32 squares 4½"
Nine-Patch	4 strips 2½"	20 squares 2½" 10 rectangles 2½" x 6½"
Medium Pink ⅝ yd.		
Connector B	1 strip 4½"	4 squares 4½"
Nine-Patch	4 strips 2½"	24 squares 2½" 12 rectangles 2½" x 6½"
Dark Pink ⅝ yd.		
Connector B	2 strips 4½"	12 squares 4½"
Nine-Patch	4 strips 2½"	36 squares 2½" 8 rectangles 2½" x 6½"

Backing 5½ yd. 2 panels 35" x 92" or 6 yds. for 3 panels 33" x 68"

Batting 68" x 92"

Block Assembly

Plain Blocks

make 40

Connector Blocks

| make 4 | make 12 | make 4 |

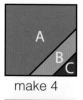

| make 4 | make 4 | make 8 |

| make 8 | make 4 | make 4 |

Nine-Patch Blocks

| make 4 | make 2 | make 4 | make 4 |

| make 4 | make 2 | make 2 | make 4 |

  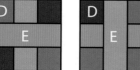

| make 4 | make 4 | make 4 | make 4 |

  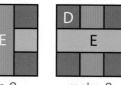

| make 4 | make 4 | make 4 | make 4 |

| make 4 | make 4 | make 4 |

| make 4 | make 2 |

1. Paying close attention to color placement, make all the blocks shown in the block assembly diagrams.

2. Spray the blocks with sizing and press. The sewn blocks should measure 6½" square. (Block assembly instructions begin on page 40.)

Quilt Assembly

Rotation

1. To make it easier to arrange the blocks and see that they are positioned correctly, lay out and sew a half of the design at a time. Then sew the halves together to complete the quilt top.

2. Layer the quilt top with batting and backing; baste. Quilt the layers (see quilting ideas on page 43). Bind the raw edges and label your quilt.

Half quilt (make 2)

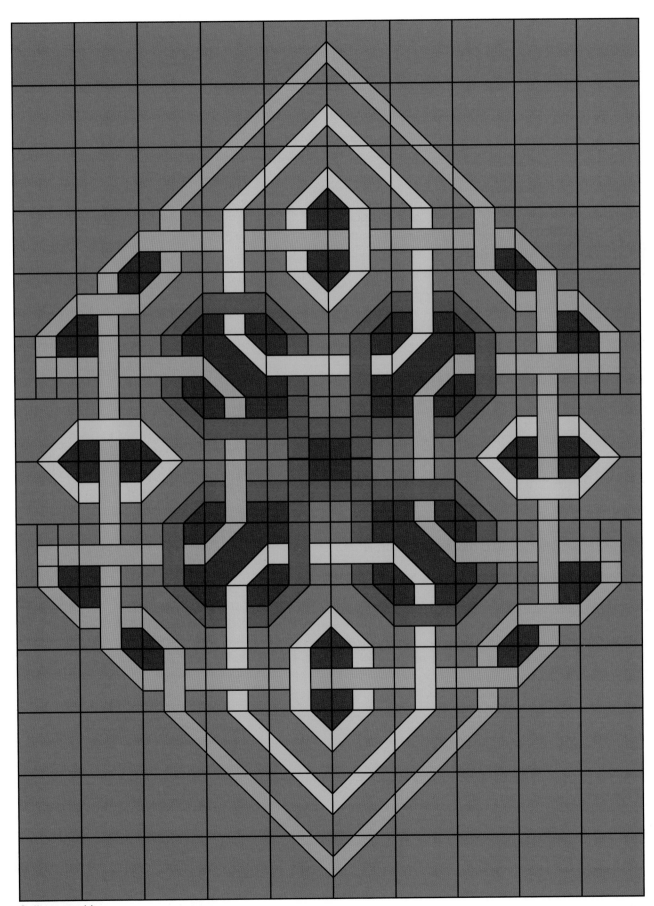

Quilt assembly

For Quilt Teachers

The ideas and quilts in this book are ideal for multi-week classes or an all-day, six-hour class. You will find class descriptions, class outlines, supply lists, and other ideas for each class format to help make a class successful.

Promoting the Class

The most valuable promotion for a class held in a quilt shop is a good sample of the class project. Make sure the sample is attractive and well constructed. It should be displayed in a highly visible area, not hung in a dark corner. Another valuable tool is a flyer, and many shops mail a newsletter listing classes, sales, interesting products, and other information. Use the following class descriptions to increase interest in the class.

Six-Hour Class (description for shop newsletter)

Celtic Charm Quilt

Do you love Celtic designs but would rather piece than appliqué? We have the perfect quilt for you! Create CELTIC CHARM, an intriguing pieced Celtic design from Karen Comb's book *Celtic Pieced Illusions*. You won't believe how easy it is to make this charming quilt.

Multi-week Class (description for shop newsletter)

Celtic Patchwork Illusions

Do you love Celtic designs, but would rather piece than appliqué? We have the perfect technique for you! Learn to design and sew your own Celtic creation from Karen Combs' book *Celtic Pieced Illusions*. You won't believe how easy it is to make these charming quilts.

Class Goals

During class, students will learn to
- select fabric
- properly rotary-cut shapes
- sew with an accurate ¼" seam allowance
- correctly match seams
- understand numerous design possibilities
- finish a wallhanging in class, or a big quilt at home
- plan a quilting design and learn how to bind a quilt

Class Size

Consider the classroom size and the instructor's experience before deciding how many students to accept into a class. Twenty students is probably the largest class size to consider. If your classroom is small, I would suggest no more than eight to a class.

Class Length

This technique is perfect for a class that meets once a week for four weeks or for a one-time, all-day workshop.

It is important to meet with students before class to select fabrics. During this meeting, they can use pre-selected colors based on the pattern on page 52, or they can select their own colors. If you don't want to meet before class, I suggest preparing kits for purchase when they sign up for class.

Classroom Setup

I suggest no more than two students to a table. Each student will need room for a sewing machine, cutting surface, and a design surface. Each student should have access to her own design wall. The design wall (a piece of flannel or even cotton batting) can be taped to the wall and taken home at the end of each class. Four, or fewer, students for each ironing surface is ideal. Be careful, irons use a great deal of electricity. If you are in an old building, you could blow a fuse. Check this out before scheduling the class. Also make sure there are adequate outlets. If not, you may need to provide power strips and extension cords.

Supplies

A supply list can be given to students when they sign up for the class, or the list can be printed in a newsletter or flyer. To respect the copyright laws, do not make photocopies of the illustrations or quilt patterns from this book or any other. Rather, require that students purchase their own books before class, or the cost of the book can be added to the workshop fee.

Student Supply List (six-hour class)
Celtic Pieced Illusions book
rotary cutter and cutting mat
rotary rulers (6" x 12" and 6½" x 6½")
sewing machine threaded with light gray thread
seam ripper
sharp pencil
one yard of flannel for a design wall
tape to hang design wall
can of sizing
fabrics for CELTIC CHARM quilt (page 52)

Student Supply List (four-week class)
Celtic Pieced Illusions book
rotary cutter and cutting mat
rotary rulers (6" x 12" and 6½" x 6½")
sewing machine threaded with light gray thread
paper scissors
seam ripper
sharp pencil
glue stick
one yard of flannel for a design wall
tape to hang design wall
can of sizing
fabrics for CELTIC CHARM quilt (page 52)

Teacher's Supply List
rotary cutter and cutting mat
rotary rulers (6" x 12" and 6½" x 6½")
handouts and samples
Celtic Pieced Illusions book
sewing machine threaded with neutral thread
basic sewing supplies

Suggestions for Teachers
• Bring a nametag for each student.
• Arrive at least 40 minutes early to set up the classroom because many students come early.
• Encourage questions. There are no dumb questions.
• If possible, give equal time to each student.
• Gently suggest how to correct mistakes and always point out the positive first.

• Class is not the time for the instructor to tell students about personal problems.
• If a student starts talking about personal issues, gently guide the class back to the fun of quilting.
• The instructor should have a positive attitude and speak in a cheerful, upbeat manner.
• An instructor should never teach a technique she has not tried.

Six-Hour Class Format

• Mist fabrics with sizing before cutting.
• Demonstrate rotary cutting for strips and squares.
• Follow the cutting chart (page 53), to cut squares.
• Lay out the Nine-Patch blocks.
• Demonstrate sewing sequence for Nine-Patch blocks.
• Make Nine-Patch blocks.
• Lay out the Connector blocks.
• Demonstrate making Connector blocks.
• Lay out the quilt and sew the blocks together, making sure to show proper pinning techniques.

Weekly Class Format

Session One

Emphasis designing a quilt by using the techniques shown in *Celtic Pieced Illusions*.

Design options: print several 6 x 6 grids and basic blocks for each student.

Demonstrate how to lay out Nine-Patch blocks and Connector blocks to create different designs. Allow time for students to play with this concept.

Adding color and illusion: print out several copies of figure 2-3 for each student. It is located on page 23.

Demonstrate how to use color to create transparency and make the cables look woven. Allow time for students to play with this technique.

Homework: have students play with these techniques. Before class two, they will need to select their favorite design and add color to it.

Session Two

Show students how to figure their block and yardage needs. Have them buy fabric during this session.

Print out a quilt design sheet (p. 35) for each student. Help students paste their final quilt design onto the sheet and color in the blocks. Double-check their drawings. Print out a cutting chart for each student, located on page 37. Demonstrate how to fill in the chart. Double-check their work.

Using the chart, determine the yardage for the quilt. Help students pick out fabrics, following their charts.

Homework: Students should cut out squares, following their cutting charts.

Session Three

Demonstrate the sewing sequence for Nine-Patch blocks. Demonstrate the sewing and trimming sequence for Connector blocks. It would be helpful to have students sew a sample Connector block.

Homework: sew Nine-Patch and Connector blocks, following their design.

Session Four

Demonstrate pinning techniques. Sew the blocks into rows. Sew rows together. Suggest quilting options. Show students how to bind a quilt.

Resources

Blank Quilting
212-563-6225
www.blankquilting.com
Manufacturer of fine quilting fabrics, including collections by Karen Combs

Connecting Threads
1-800-574-6454
www.connectingthreads.com
Fabric and notions

Hancock's of Paducah
3841 Hinkleville Road
Paducah, KY 42001
800-845-8723
www.hancocks-paducah.com
Fabric and notions

Karen Combs Studio
www.karencombs.com
Online catalog: Fabric designed by Karen Combs; supplies, workshops, and lectures by Karen Combs

Keepsake Quilting
R 25 B
Centre Harbor, NH 03226
800-525-8086
www.keepsakequilting.com
Fabric and notions

Quilt University
www.quiltuniversity.com
Online quilting classes by Karen Combs

Terry Dramstad
Quilts, Ink.
701-797-3350
Machine quilting

The Stencil Company
Fax: 716-668-2488
Email: info@quiltingstencils.com
www.quiltingstencils.com
Quilting stencils

Meet the Author

Karen Combs is an internationally known quilter, teacher, author, and designer, who has been nominated by students for Quilt Teacher of the Year in 1995, 2000, and 2005. Teaching since 1989, she is in high demand as a teacher who encourages her students, makes learning fun, and makes the complex easy to understand.

Karen is fascinated with optical illusions and quilts; this is the subject of many of her workshops, magazine articles, and books. Her quilts have appeared in the Hoffman Challenge and in many popular quilting magazines. She has appeared on several television quilting shows, among them *Quilting from the Heartland, Simply Quilts, Quilt Central, and American Quilter.*

She lives in the rolling hills of middle Tennessee with her husband Rick and a very sweet Shih Tzu named Cocoa. Karen and Rick have two grown children: Angela and Joshua. Her hobbies, besides quilting, include reading, yoga, Pilates, power walking, and American Sign Language.

She is the author of these AQS books: *Optical Illusions for Quilters, Combing Through Your Scraps,* and *Floral Illusions for Quilters,* and she is the co-author of *3 Quilters Celebrate the 4 Seasons. Celtic Pieced Illusions* is Karen's fifth book with the American Quilter's Society.

Other AQS Books

This is only a small selection of the books available from the American Quilter's Society. AQS books are known worldwide for timely topics, clear writing, beautiful color photos, and accurate illustrations and patterns. The following books are available from your local bookseller, quilt shop, or public library.

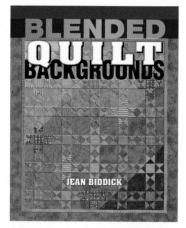

#7078   us$24.95

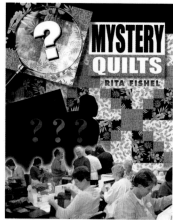

#7079   us$22.95

#4995   us$19.95

#6905   us$24.95

#6899   us$21.95

#6799   us$22.95

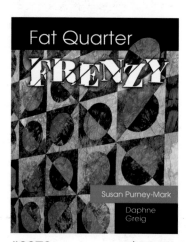

#6673   us$21.95

#6802   us$21.95

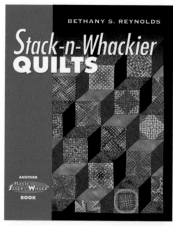

#5850   us$21.95

Look for these books nationally.
Call or **Visit** our Web site at

1-800-626-5420

www.AmericanQuilter.com